# THE ORIGIN OF RELIGION AND ITS IMPACT ON THE HUMAN SOUL

## Past Shock Part Two

By Jack Barranger

# THE BOOK TREE
### San Diego, California

The Origin of Religion and Its Impact on the Human Soul
Past Shock Part Two

© 2008
by Jack Barranger

ISBN 978-1-58509-113-3

Cover layout & design: Atulya
Interior layout and design: Atulya
Editor: Kimberly Dillon

Printed in USA on Acid-Free Paper

Published by
**The Book Tree**
P O Box 16476
San Diego, CA 92176
www.thebooktree.com

We provide fascinating and educational products to help awaken the public to new ideas and information that would not be available otherwise.
Call 1 (800) 700-8733 for our *FREE BOOK TREE CATALOG*.

# CONTENTS

# A Word to the Reader

While this book can be read as a separate entity, you will benefit greatly if you have read the first book in this series, *Past Shock*. In Appendix A at the end of the book is a summary of that work. I have two suggestions. If you have not already read the book *Past Shock*: (1) go to the end of the book now and read Appendix A; that way you will be better prepared for the reading of this book or (2) buy the book *Past Shock* and read it first. It is a short book and, if you will forgive my lack of humility, a good read. That way two things will happen: (1) you will gain a greater satisfaction from reading this book and have an even greater preparation for it and (2) if enough people take this suggestion, I will be better able to afford those lobster dinners at Red Lobster.

If you call The Book Tree 1-800-700-TREE and purchase *Past Shock* directly from the publisher, you will have it in a matter of days. It can also be found on www.amazon.com.

# Overview

    *The Origin of Religion...* is meant to keep an anchor on the ideas developed in *Past Shock* and move forward with new material. As I began giving lectures and book signings about *Past Shock*, I realized that people were just as interested in *present shock* as they were *past shock*. I was thanked for linking present problems with ancient religious conditioning. I was thanked for helping people deal with their doubts about aspects of their present religion and the holy books of those religions. What I was also asked about was how much of this was going on and how it affects areas other than religion.

    I had touched on this in the last two chapters of *Past Shock*. I knew when I was writing the book that our past shock conditioning impacted many more areas in the present than modern organized religion. I touched on its impact on work, education, and other secular areas. However, as I began appearing on radio shows and giving lectures, I realized that *Past Shock* touched many more areas than I had previously thought.

    What came out of this increasing realization was the embryo of a book taking the ideas of *Past Shock* into millennial times—the end of the one now passed and the beginning of the next one. Just as the previous millennium "prophets" terrified and manipulated people in the name of God, that same control mechanism exists, but it is no longer done just in the name of God. This manipulation has spread in the name of new age thinking, Native American spirituality, and the hordes of secular people who keep retranslating the 16th Century physician/prophet Nostradamus. The pretender gods began this manipulation. Because of their technological advancement, they had a fair amount of accuracy in predicting a flood, and yet they told only seven humans, according to the *Old Testament* and the ancient Sumerian book the *Atra-hasis*.

Five thousand years ago, it was the prophets appointed by the pretender gods who attempted to control their followers. As with the recent millennial times, and with all the excitement over the 2012 prophecies, most of the prophets appoint themselves—and they do very well, if one thinks only about money instead of accuracy.

I remembered an eleven-week summer vacation I spent researching alien abductions. I found that despite claims to the contrary, these events were, in all liklihood, genuine. With horror I saw that the fallout of past shock took a grotesque form. Most abductees I encountered were paying homage to aliens who had mentally and physically abused them. The abductees themselves were taking on the role of priest or prophet by manipulating people with claims that the aliens had told them the fate of the earth, as well telling us what to do as a way to escape or avoid it.

A term that I had never used in *Past Shock* kept forcing itself into my awareness: spiritual tyranny. Other humans, in the name of God, higher consciousness, enlightenment, and that innocuous of terms, "growth", are continuing to control those who are trying to grow in these ways. This does not in any way suggest that people who seek the above mentioned goals are fools. It is just that vultures wait out there to control and tyrannize people in the name of these worthy goals.

In *The Origin of Religion...,* I will introduce the concept of the "malfunctioning messiah"—people with a messiah complex who want to save the world but cannot even save themselves. Thirty years ago, few would have taken these unhealed healers seriously. Now people are lining up with these malfunctioning messiahs for the right to be spiritual slaves.

The malfunctioning messiah is out of control, but desperately seeks to control others. Whether he or she is part of organized religion or the new age movement, they think they have something everyone needs. Other people must have it or hell awaits, spiritual poverty will be a part of life, or a life of high limitation will hew the rest of their life.

At least Enki, Enlil, and Jehovah didn't claim to their created slaves that they were failing God if they weren't rich. Yet some of the present-day malfunctioning messiahs are pushing a prosperity con in the name of prosperity consciousness.

Even the secular success books, seminars, and weekend work-shops are using some of the tactics of the ancient pretender gods. I have interviewed people who would rouse and chant far beyond the zeal and noise of a Pentecostal church. I have actually watched thirteen people gang up on one person and humiliate him for an hour and a half telling him that his consciousness was so low that he wouldn't succeed at much of anything in life. This, of course, was all done in the name of love and the desire to help. Everyone hugged one another at the end of this session.

At least 5,000 years ago a warlord declared himself to be God and made it really hot for anyone who failed to comply or conform. Then, it was about worshiping Jehovah and only Jehovah, as well as working hard with little reward. Eventually it was about fighting wars for the lazy warlords.

Could this haranguing for an hour and a half been a reflection of when Jehovah harangued his starving and desert-weary Israelites for daring to be incompliant or not live up to his expectations? Could the affect of having thousands of poisonous snakes thrown into their midst still have an impact on people even now?

This and much more is happening today, thanks to the condi-tioning the emerging human race received thousands of years ago.

# Glossary

## Terms Used in This Book

I get especially angry with people in organizations who use "in" buzzwords in a manner that reinforces their "in-ness." Take, for example, multicultural fanatics on college campuses who use the term DWEM, which means Dead White European Male. All of a sudden someone eighteen years old at a politically correct university has a smug term that inflates the ego of the person using the term and trivializes the accomplishments of white European Males, who, in these politically correct times, may be lucky to be on the other side.

After making the questionable spiritual decision of accepting Jesus as my personal savior at age 13, I was "joyfully" introduced to the term *baby Christain*. I don't ever remember this term being used in love or outside the restrictions of spiritual manipulation. If I said something deemed to be spiritually incorrect, I was told that this was what was expected from a baby Christian. I tried to introduce the term *old fart Christian*, but that one never caught on.

What follows are terms used in this book. I don't expect anyone to take them as gospel, and I pray that they never become "in." The terms and their short explanation are meant to *clarify* rather than manipulate. Nor do I expect everyone to believe the foundation of these created terms, as I have found them. That would be stepping on your spiritual freedom.

**Archetype** — a term invented by the Swiss psychologist Carl Gustav Jung, meaning a racial memory from the past that still impacts humanity today. Common archetypes known today are the dedicated mother, the warrior hero, and the one leaving home to discover the world. Lesser-known forms of archetypes are the tricksters, the belief in God, and the crucified and resurrected savior. (According to ancient myth, there were 17 crucified and resurrected saviors throughout history,

8

including Jesus.) Archetypes are part of what Jung referred to as the collective unconscious—meaning that they are deeply inside our experience and impact us unconsciously and consciously today.

**Anunnaki** — from the ancient Sumerian language meaning "those who from heaven came." Zecharia Sitchin and others feel that these were extraterrestrial beings from the planet Nibiru, which is four times the size of earth and circles earth in extreme ellipsis, coming into our solar system once every 3,600 years. British researcher Christian O'Brien believes that the Anunnaki were highly technological beings who "came from the high plains." Author Rene Boulay feels that they were reptilian and cites convincing verses from Sumerian literature and the Old Testament to support this. Wherever they came from, they were primarily mean and treated the human race brutally.

**Enki** — one of the two main Sumerian gods who, by default to his mean-spirited brother Enlil, was considered to be a more compassionate god. His greatest act of compassion was warning Utnapishtam (Noah) that a mighty flood was coming and that he should build an ark to save himself, six other people, and a host of animals from the flood. According to Sumerian and some Native American Indian legends, Enki also was the creator of the human race. Some mythological scholars claimed that Enki was the serpent in the Garden of Eden. In the *Epic of Gilgamesh* and other places he is referred to as Ea.

**Enlil** — an s.o.b. if there ever was one. Other than Anu ("the most high") Enlil was the main Sumerian god. He gave the command to "create" the human race as a worker/slave force by combining their DNA with that of the Neanderthal species. His only purpose for this creation was to prevent a mutiny by the Anunnaki (see above), who had come here for the mining of gold and minerals, and needed a worker race to replace them in their work. Enlil also decided to end this entire new creation when he felt their ranks were growing too fast and their constant wailing deprived him of sleep. His only recorded moment of compassion was beginning to weep when he saw—from a spaceship—millions of people frantically drowning in the flood.

Immediately Enlil flew into a rage, however, when Enki told him that he had saved seven of the worker/slave force.

**Godspell** — a term coined by author Neil Freer in his book *Breaking the Godspell* and continued in his latest book *God Games*. A godspell is a "spell" ancient humans were put under through DNA manipulation to make them work hard for their creator gods and eventually to worship them as the true God of the Universe. I also refer to this as the "slave chip" (see below), when combined with the heavy conditioning that we as a race were subjected to.

**Jehovah** — a stentorian warlord, also known as Yahweh, who took the emerging Israelites into the desert for forty years and trained them to be warriors. Among his many crimes was claiming to be the true God. People who didn't believe this were punished harshly. Other crimes were training his warriors to commit genocide on innocent people who were deemed guilty by Jehovah. Two times in the Old Testament either Moses and Pharaoh or the Hivites and Joshua had made peace with each other, and Jehovah hardened their hearts so they would fight, allowing Jehovah to have his glory. For reasons beyond human understanding, he brought plagues and famines to his own people. He was (and still remains) one of the most overrated figures in ancient history.

**Ninhirsag** — the Sumerian goddess who allowed the genetically engineered species to be placed in her womb. She was known as the first mother goddess. Sumerian texts tell us that a number of genetically defective offspring first occurred before they finally succeeded. According to Sumerian holy books and historical accounts, Ninhirsag is the mother of humanity.

**Past Shock** — As the foundation for the book *Past Shock,* past shock is the collected impact of the fallout from brutal wars fought in God's name, the brutal treatment of worker/slaves, and the eventual conditioning of humans thousands of years ago to believe that the gods of the past were true gods. This conditioning still survives today because people refuse to face it. This conditioning creates workaholics, religious fanatics at all levels, new age gurus who dominate their people rather than liberate them, and the ability to solve problems and gain particular political favor by going to war rather than making peace.

**The Pretender Gods** — a term that I used liberally in my book *Past Shock*. The "Pretender Gods" were technologically advanced beings that were here as late as 800 BCE. Some claimed these were mythological figures; others, like author Zecharia Sitchin, claimed that they were real physical beings who were more than likely not human. These Pretender Gods did exactly what their name suggests; they pretended to be God. The evidence points very strongly to the fact that they genetically engineered Neanderthal man into Cro-Magnon man and therefore claimed credit for creating us. Because they "created us," they assumed that they had the right to be worshipped as "God." Most of humanity has understandably bought into this lie, preventing others from experiencing the True God.

**Ruling Priest Class** — those who were appointed to be priests and speak for the Pretender Gods. In the beginning, these were the Sumerian and Egyptian priest/kings, and the prophets of the *Old Testament*. In *New Testament* times they were groups like the Pharisees and the Sandhedrin. Today, the role is sadly dominated by self-appointed gurus, and church and spiritual leaders who choose to control rather than edify.

**Slave Chip** — the conditioning the Pretender Gods inflicted on us in combination with our genetic tampering and "creation", which reinforces our slave mentality. It made us worship them as true gods, although others have come in to take their place (see Ruling Priest Class, above).

**Spiritually Correct** — an allusion to the "politically correct" movement budding in the 1990's, which is an attempt to limit free expression of speech because it is considered offensive or in poor taste. *Spiritually correct* embraces the same insanity except that it centers on religious and spiritual matters. Despite increases in evidence that Jesus might have been married, the idea is not spiritually correct; therefore it is rarely discussed. Salmund Rushdie's gentle satire of Islam's founder Mohammed was considered so spiritually incorrect that Islamic leaders put out a "spiritual hit" called a "fatwah" on Rushdie. Evidently, love and forgiveness are not yet spiritually correct. When used in this book, the term is meant to be sarcastic—suggesting that some spiritual consensus reality is superior to personal spiritual freedom.

**Spiritual Tyranny** — my coined term, meaning one human's interference with another person's right to embrace—or ignore—a higher power in the manner they choose. History's greatest example of spiritual tyranny was the Spanish Inquisition when the Roman Catholic Church exerted its power for 300 years, putting people who didn't have the "correct" belief systems in prison, burned at a fiery stake, or in the torture chamber. More modern examples of spiritual tyranny are the killing and harassment of doctors who perform abortions, the cajoling of people who no longer believe the religion they grew up with, and the controlling behavior of some new age gurus, who believe that haranguing and harassment are okay as long as they achieve the desired results: enlightenment, higher consciousness, a great deal of money, more converts, recognition, or the spreading or acceptance of their narrow version of spiritual freedom.

**The true God** — in *Past Shock,* I came to the conclusion that many figures who claimed to be God [Jehovah, Zeus, Ba'al, etc.] were instead pretenders (see "The Pretender Gods" ). The *true God* is the creator of souls at a level far beyond the physical level. The *true God* wants people to be free. However, the *true God* does not function on the physical level, where most people are looking, but instead leaves it to the High Self or Holy Spirit. We can find the *true God*, if we know how to look beyond the physical for our answers.

*Chapter One*

# The Impact of Eden

## The Two Main Views of the Garden of Eden

The first version of the Garden of Eden experience is that which is conditioned into most Jews and Christians. It states that Adam was alone and had a helpmate created for him. Both tilled the Garden and could have whatever they wanted, except for the fruit from the tree in the middle of the Garden—the Tree of Knowledge.

From this perspective, bad girl Eve ate some of the fruit and then offered it to Adam. Both were naked and immediately felt shame. God compounded this shame with his rage, casting both out of the Garden of Eden with three harsh additions:

> 1. Women would bear children in pain,
> 2. Men would work by the sweat of their brow, and
> 3. Conflict would ensue between men and women.

To drive the point home, fiery angels were placed at the entrance of Eden to prevent Adam and Eve from getting back in.

The other version of the Garden of Eden is much safer: the Adam and Eve story is a myth. This myth is a teaching story, much like the Greek myth of Icarus. Icarus wanted to fly and made wings from wax and bird feathers, which he attached to his arms. As he was flying he accidentally got too close to the sun. The wax on his wings began to melt, and Icarus crashed into the sea.

13

Thus, the Garden of Eden is a warning myth. Icarus flew too high and crashed into the sea; Adam and Eve ate of the Tree of Knowledge and were tossed from the Garden. Throw in the tale of Prometheus stealing fire from the gods, giving it to humanity, and then being severely punished, and we have some myths that send out a concerning message:

> Learning too much can bring dire consequences.

As a college teacher I can tell you that we don't have to worry about students learning too much in the United States. In the past thirty years a college degree has descended in gained knowledge to what used to constitute a high school diploma. Both students and colleagues pressure teachers who want educational excellence from their students into lowing their standards.

A dumbing down of epic proportions is going on in America; few will doubt that. What the majority of people fail to realize is that the dumbing down began in the Garden of Eden and is one of the most horrendous impacts of humanity's past shock.

Think of the expressions that are a part of American English. What does a teacher say to a student who is out of line: "Don't get smart with me." A parent will use the expression, "You're too smart for your own good" to indicate that a child has gone too far in some action or speech. Maybe this child was a reincarnation of Adam or Icarus.

Thirty years ago, the expression "wise-guy" didn't have just the Mafia connotation. "Don't be a wise-guy" meant that you were too smart for your own good. "Wise up" is sometimes said to mean to dumb down. It can also mean, "Stop what you're doing right now"— like flying or eating of the Tree of Knowledge.

The Garden of Eden as a myth allows scholars to avoid the impact of one of the most devastating moments in human history.

The Garden of Eden story is not a fictional story. It happened. However, it wasn't God who threw and Eve out of the Garden of Eden, nor was it God who told them not to eat of the Tree of Knowledge. It also wasn't Satan, Lucifer, or the devil that urged Adam and Eve to eat of the fruit.

The one who demanded that Adam and Eve not eat of the Tree of Knowledge was either Jehovah or the Elohim. Jehovah was a war-lord who declared himself to be God to the emerging human race. The Elohim was a race of technologically superior beings that "created" humanity. The Elohim was not God or anything close to it.

The Serpent was not an evil creature. It wanted the liberation of Adam and Eve because it saw that humans were being treated like worker/slaves and cosmic pets instead of being encouraged to advance mentally and spiritually. The Serpent also may have been more than one person. In *The Gods of Eden,* William Bramley mentions a group that secretly attempted to advance humanity. They were called The Brotherhood of the Snake:

> The group was a discipline Brotherhood dedi-
> cated to the dissemination of spiritual knowl-
> edge and attainment of spiritual freedom. The
> Brotherhood of the Snake... opposed the
> enslavement of spiritual beings and according
> to Egyptian writings, it sought to liberate the
> human race from Custodial bondage. The
> Brotherhood also imparted scientific knowl-
> edge and encouraged the high aesthetics that
> existed in many ancient societies.

In his book Bramley also referred to the Elohim or the early controlling gods as the "Custodians", hence the term "Custodial bondage". For thousands of years we have been viewing those who spiritually raped us as the good guys and those who tried to set us free as the bad guys. This creates spiritual confusion and prevents spiritual liberation. If the good guys are those who enslaved us, then all attempts at spiritual freedom will be seen as an act against God.

This is where we stand in the world today. In the structure of the three main world religions, spiritual freedom is only allowed if you stay within the extremely limited parameters of that religion's dogmas. Not a very pleasant—or liberating—prospect.

## The Serpent as Liberator

Most people are so highly conditioned to think of the Serpent as evil that overcoming this conditioning and considering it as a liberating form is difficult for most people in the Western world. This conditioning works even at the cellular level; some people experience absolute terror of a snake despite the fact that a snake has never harmed them. Many young children cringe in horror the first time they see a snake. Our creators conditioned us well.

Some traits about the Serpent are worth exploring. First of all, simply stated, the Serpent never insisted on being worshipped.

Secondly, the Serpent is the bringer of knowledge, not the prohibitor. From the "Haggadah", one of the contemporary texts of the Old Testament, comes a more detailed account of the Serpent's explanation to Adam and Even about the Tree of Knowledge. The Serpent has urged Adam and Eve to touch the Tree of Knowledge:

> You see that touching the tree has not caused your death. As little will it hurt you to eat of the fruit of the tree. Naught but malevolence has prompted the prohibition, for as soon as you eat thereof, you shall be as Gods [the Elohim].... He himself ate of the fruit of the tree, and then he created the world. Therefore, he forbids you to eat lest you create other worlds.

This is a much more thorough version than the Genesis account of the so called "fall of man." The Serpent is telling Adam and Eve that they can be co-creators with the Elohim. While the true God has no problem with humans being co-creators with God, the Elohim didn't want this at all. They wanted a worker/slave race that would work, fight for, and worship them.

It was not the Serpent who treated Jehovah brutally but instead Jehovah who treated the Serpent brutally.

The Serpent was most likely Enki, the one god who sided with humans more than all the others. The one who warned Adam and Eve not to eat of the fruit of the tree was most likely Enlil (who later became Jehovah). Enki was telling the truth and Enlil was lying.

**The Birth of Shame and Guilt**

No one can tell for sure when guilt or shame was born. However, Genesis 3 is the first time that shame or guilt is mentioned in the Old Testament. Once Adam and Eve had eaten of the Tree of Knowledge, they noticed for the first time that they were naked and they felt shame. The "Haggadah" adds an interesting twist:

> The first result was that Adam and Eve became naked. Before, their bodies had been overlaid with a horny skin and enveloped with a horny skin... and the horny skin dropped from them and they stood there in their naked-ness and ashamed.

What is this shame? And what is this horny skin? Could it have been that Adam and Eve's experience was more like a snake shedding its skin? If so, could they have felt so vulnerable that it could have been interpreted as shame? In the human experience, no one feels shame about his or her body until it is conditioned into them. The shame is not a natural part of us. We have to be conditioned into believing that being naked is shameful.

Thanks to this conditioning, web sites all over the world are springing up to allow "shameful" people to see what is forbidden. Regardin this shame, just walk into the wrong restroom and notice the shock—this is rhetorical and not suggested. No body parts are seen, but fear erupts. The person walking in by mistake feels intensely embarrassed. He had no intention of seeing anything. Good God, he can see whatever he wants on the Internet. Something deeper is going on, and it most likely began at Eden.

I once observed something pertaining to this when living in Michigan. A very religious woman clothed her male dog like a person so that its testes and genitals could not be seen. This well trained dog had to first be disrobed, then go into a closed off area to defecate and urinate, and then its clothes were put back on. Just as this woman had trained her dog to feel guilt when he defecated on the rug, so was she successful in training the dog to feel shame when he was not clothed. The dog would not leave the house until it had its diaper on. When a teasing teenager pulled off the diaper, the dog bit the offender and scurried quickly and shamefully home.

This is the only example I know of a dog feeling shame about its genitals being exposed. Almost all animals are just fine being naked; so are children until family members pass on the "shame value." Some families try very hard to avoid conditioning their children this way. However, the shame of others provides a pressure to conform to the shame and guilt conditioning.

We did not need this shame then.

We don't need this shame now.

Shame in ancient times and modern is not something natural; it had to be conditioned. In the same way that some humans housebreak dogs, so were the ancient humans conditioned to feel shame about nothing that was shameful.

I have students tell me that they are ashamed if they begin thinking that the religion of their birth may not be true.

I have had friends who feel guilty because they begin to doubt whether the Bible is the word of God.

Even more extreme are people who feel guilty if they don't read the Bible every day.

In all three examples, the guilt is not something natural. It is something that had to be conditioned into the human experience. Guilt, shame, and remorse have no place in the human experience. Four times in my life I have accidentally walked into the ladies room. Each time I apologized and exited. However, screams, indignation, and even an exhortation of, "Get the hell out of here!" did not cause me to feel shame or guilt. Momentary embarrassment, yes. Regret, yes. But I intended no wrong, and therefore felt no guilt. However, in two of the incidents women followed me out and tried to make me feel guilty.

So it was with Jehovah. He put the Tree of Knowledge right in the middle of the garden and then expected Adam and Eve to avoid it. As we will explore later in this chapter, it's possible that Adam and Eve were set up.

If guilt began with the Garden of Eden experience, it runs deep in modern times:

In Stalin's 1936 purge of past leaders, high ranking officers rushed forward to confess to crimes they never committed.

During the horrific 1950's McCarthy trials, people felt guilty for going to a group meeting—but not until it had been labeled a communist front organization. They didn't feel guilty or have any desire to explore communist or socialist ideas when they went to the meeting. It was not until the McCarthy hearings that the guilt and ensuing confessions came from some people.

The guilt over masturbation is conditioned into people, whether from religious or cultural conditioning. Monkeys, gorillas, and apes masturbate freely—even when surrounded by people in the captivity of the zoo. No one is conditioning the simians; they have no religion to restrict them or culture that forbids it.

Guilt impacts the human experience. In junior high school I had been well conditioned to feel guilt when I got a low grade. However, that didn't stop me from failing two of the three grades of junior high school.

Conditioning takes interesting turns in relation to a woman getting pregnant outside of marriage. I live in Tulare County, California, which has the doubtful distinction of being the unwed mother capital of the United States. Still, in the 1990's I observed the guilt that some women felt. It is thanks to the patriarchal society that has existed for the past five thousand years that woman feels such guilt. Have you ever heard of a man getting in trouble for making a woman pregnant? Because of this ancient patriarchal conditioning, it is even the female rape victim that often feels more shame and guilt than her male rapist.

## Give Me That Old Time Conditioning

Thanks to our conditioning we feel guilty far in excess of any transgression. The man who calls in sick for a minimum wage job feels much more guilt than someone making ten times what he does and takes off four hours to play golf. The first man is genuinely ill; the person playing golf is just fine.

This inequality of guilt to transgression must have come from the time of building pyramids and mining for minerals. The Anunnaki, the Elohim, or Jehovah himself caused guilt by ranting and raving. Punishment far in excess of the crime was used as an effective way to stimulate both fear and guilt.

If you feel sick working the mines, you ignore it and push harder because you've been conditioned to want to be a good worker, and feel guilty if you're not. Feel sick working at the office, and you will be tempted to push harder. If you really are sick, perhaps a day or two off fits within the paradigm. However, taking the doctor's orders and staying in bed for a week is out of the question. Doing so could cause guilt—not to mention being "out of the swim" of the competition.

Likewise, depart from believing that Jehovah was the true God, and forces from Jehovah and his followers brought great guilt— and pain.

Depart from believing that the cult you are in is the true faith and people will make you feel guilty. With some of the cults, the conditioning is ingenious. Say the right things, and the group will roar with approval. Express doubt about a cult issue, and the approval is withdrawn. Since most modern humans want approval—and certainly want to avoid guilt—the conditioning is well planned and very effective.

Why is this so effective in cults? Because cult leaders and some of their disciples have latched onto a way to tap into that ancient guilt and use it for their aims.

Programmed guilt goes deep into the human mind. I saw an excellent example of this at a Thanksgiving dinner when a four-year-old girl ran up and greeted a relative with a big hug. In her excitement she peed her pants and got some on the uncle she hadn't seen for a year. She was immediately filled with shame, and ran from the room crying. A half hour later she was still in the bathroom crying. She was so full of shame that she didn't want to see anyone—including her uncle.

When the uncle finally got her to talk, he realized that her father had punished her severely for wetting the bed and those other very rare times that she lost control. He had harangued her, claiming that she was a big girl and that big girls don't make mistakes like that.

Though the mother was no longer married to the father and the father wasn't present, the impact of the conditioning still remained. An hour and a half later she still didn't want to go near the uncle. Her shame was immeasurable.

Notice that the father wasn't even there. I was told that he had an angry look that cut like a laser beam, and although he wasn't there, her conditioning was. The same is true of the shame and conditioning that has been programmed into us from thousands of years ago. We still have the shame, but the producer of the shame is long gone. The pretender gods who conditioned us so well are no longer here, yet the shame and guilt remains.

### The Slave Chip and Guilt

One working hypothesis is that guilt was part of the conditioning used to create such a powerful slave chip. It was so successful that it is in good working condition 2,800 years after most of the pretender gods have departed.

The Garden of Eden must have been a devastating experience for humanity. Because of the intensity of what Adam and Eve experienced and had to watch, the impact had to be severe—and perhaps right along with what Jehovah had intended.

Consider the brutal punishments that were lashed down upon Adam, Eve, and the Serpent.

**First,** both Adam and Eve were told that there would be a forced antagonism between them. What good could this possibly serve except to create both shame and guilt that would work for more effective conditioning?

**Second,** Eve was told that she—and all other women—would have to bear children in pain and suffering. What good could this possibly achieve? In having me, my mother went through an extremely painful and frightening 14-hour labor. This caused her to be so fearful that she never wanted to be pregnant again. It also deprived me of future brothers and sisters that were in Mom and Dad's plans.

Should I get angry with my mother?
Should I get angry with Eve?

Actually I am angry with Jehovah—or the Elohim—who went completely out of control and inflicted excessive punishment for what probably wasn't even a crime. Jehovah sorely needed his ass to be kicked, but there was no one around to do it. He reigned his horror freely without resistance and programmed a race to quiver in fear rather than stand with courage. I am exasperated with the people in organized religion who still feel that it is the fault of one woman and one man. This has never been proven, and if not part of the Old Testament, this idea would have died quickly except for one thing: the conditioning is still there.

**Third**, Adam was told that his days would be severely numbered and that he would have to work by the sweat of his brow. What a wonderful way to condition people to work even harder for their gods. Adam commits a misdemeanor and then gets to rot in the Gulag for the rest of his life.

**Fourth**, Adam and Eve have to watch the entity that was trying to set them free be brutally and painful punished—once again far in excess of the crime. The following is from the "Haggadah"

> The mouth of the serpent was closed, and his
> power of speech taken away; his hands and
> feet were hacked off.... he must suffer great
> pain in sloughing his skin.... men shall seek to
> kill him as soon as they catch sight of him.

## Present Shock

The fact that we are not horrified by these extreme measures causes wonder. The villain in this case was Jehovah. His rage was beyond his control. In the modern world this would compare to being a coach or company president raging out of control, physically and mentally abusing his employees, and blackballing them from any future work. However, this example doesn't even come close to the horrors perpetuated in the Garden of Eden.

Throughout the "Haggadah" version of the Garden of Eden story are references to Jehovah insisting that he respond tenfold for each sin. This is worse than the horrendous Covenant that Jehovah pushed on the Israelites. Any sins in the covenant would only be retaliated seven fold. Instead of seeing Jehovah as God, it is more important to see him as a brazen bully, obsessed with capturing new territory and enjoying the carnage of destroying the land, buildings, and lives of the people in this territory.

## Was the Fall Essential?

The "fall" was essential because, if not for the Serpent, humanity would have spent a much longer time being cosmic pets instead of spiritual beings. Despite its benefits, however, the "fall" was akin to breaking out of jail with no money or clothing: you're free but you're on your own, and it's kind of scary. Yet you find ways to make clothing and hunt for food. You have no choice; survival demands it. Then in the most curious of circumstances the ones who have just broken out of jail now want to go back, because for so many years that jail was their home. But the guards hold them off at gunpoint. In spite of all of this, those who were previously prisoners claim that the warden is God and all the guards are angels.

You don't want to go back to Eden.

You don't want to go home.

## Moving Beyond Eden

Home is where you are now. Focusing on returning home in some future time is part of the trap. Whether a new age doctrine or an organized religion's dogma, you are deep in the trap if you get caught up in the idea of a great reward in the future for suffering here on earth. So are those deluded who buy into processed dogma TV dinners, which you put in the oven and out comes salvation.

People who focus on guilt from the past or hope for the future are not very effective in the present moment. They languish for promises never committed to or even considered by the true God. If Jehovah is still alive—which is a good possibility—I doubt if he really cares what you do. If he did, he would not have left you to struggle on your own.

For those who claim that Jehovah sent his only begotten son to save the world, it just looks like it didn't work. Furthermore, why did Jehovah send his pure son and why did he have Jesus take on the sins of the world instead of himself? And, if humanity was saved by this act, why is humanity in the mess it's in now?

Please don't say that it was Adam and Eve's eating of the Tree of Knowledge.

## Chapter Two

# The Fallout from the Tower of Babel: Slouching Toward Humanity in the Modern Age

Three acts of the pretender gods so impacted humanity that people today are but shells of what they used to be. First was the expulsion from the Garden of Eden, replete with fiery angels and flaming swords. The trauma of this event has already been discussed—both in ancient times and its impact on people today.

Second was the flood. It happened. Modern science has now proved that this was an event that happened about 12,000 years ago. Millions of people drowning with no hope of being saved is a traumatic incident burned into our cellular memory. The pretender gods watching from above most have even felt some of the trauma. Even Enlil, who ordered the event and allowed a flood to occur without warning anyone, shed some tears as he witnessed the terror and panic below. The *Atra-hasis* records Enlil being upset as he watched the horrifying events.

Poor Enlil.

However, the events that may have had the greatest impact on the emerging human race were those surrounding the building and the destruction of the Tower of Babel. This event has not been quickly forgotten, nor is it so deeply buried that it has no present impact. We are still greatly affected by the event today, and in a very narrow way.

Since Genesis 11 is the Old Testament's only account of the Tower of Babel, we have little to work with. However, those few verses are most revealing in explaining how this was a significant moment of past shock. Verse 5 begins with obvious optimism and somewhat desirable conditions:

> Now the whole earth used only one language. On
> the occasion of a migration from the east, men dis-
> covered a plain in the land of Shinar and settled
> there. They said to one another, "Come, let us make
> bricks, burning them well."

Nothing here indicates that something evil is going on. A group
of people just completed a migration and they decide to work together on a project. This is a bonding and creative effort on the part of the
people. No one—not even the pretender gods—walks up to them and
says, "You know, this really isn't a good idea." If the project is something evil, they are not stopped. Thus, whoever is watching the project
continue is allowing the emerging humans to do something that will
eventually hurt them.

The lack of wisdom in this decision is horrifying.

They continued with their work, having no idea that they were
going to be thumped:

> So they used bricks for stone, and bitumen for mor-
> tar. Then they said, Come, let us build a tower
> whose top shall reach the heavens (this making a
> name for ourselves) so that we may not be scattered
> all over the earth.

In this verse lies one of the most overlooked clues in the Old
Testament. They want to build this tower so that they can avoid being
"scattered all over the earth." If this was a close-knit group of people,
their fear of being scattered was understandable, and they had a great
sense of purpose and community in preventing this.

Less than 150 years ago, black slaves lived in terror that their
families would be broken up. They prayed to God that one plantation
would purchase the husband, wife, and all the children. Tragically, this

didn't happen often, and husband and wife—along with the children—
would be separated, in many cases never seeing each other again.
Today we understand how horrible this is. However, in the middle of
the nineteenth century, the African slaves were treated callously
because people didn't consider them to be human.

Does this sound familiar? Isn't this exactly the way the pretender gods treated their newly created humans? This is yet another
example of the horrifying fallout of past shock.

Reading between the lines, one gets the sense that these
Babylonians eluded the watchful eyes of the pretender gods. Only the
cruelest of pretender gods would say, "Let's let them build the project
and then we'll tear it down." Most likely, some people escaped from
the clutches of the pretender gods and went undetected for a while.
This is only a theory and nothing is mentioned in the Old Testament
about this, but it is a hypothesis worth considering.

A further hint to support this hypothesis comes in the next
verse:

> And the Lord came down to see the city and the
> tower, which the children and the men had
> builded.

If the Lord God is omnipotent, omniscient, and omnipresent,
why would he *have to come down to the city and tower*? Something is
wrong with this picture. The verse hints that something is being discovered. If this is so, then whoever is making the discovery is not God.
What follows is a statement from God that is even more ungodly:

> And the Lord said, Behold the people is one and
> they have one language; and this they begin to
> do; and now nothing will be restrained from
> them, which they have imagined to do.

Let us go down and confound their language
that they may not understand each other's
speech.

How Jews and Christians can worship a God who would perform such a horrendous act is beyond my understanding. This is a
bully God. If this "God" was indeed omniscient, this "God" is worse
than a bully because he allowed people to continue with their work
until it was finished and then, with the utmost cruelty, destroyed it.
There is no compassion, respect, or wisdom in such an act. This
instead represents what the pretender gods did best—inflict cruelty on
humans who did not have the power to resist.

What in heaven's name is wrong with being "one people" and
understanding "each other's speech"? How could a loving and compassionate god be threatened by something like this? The true God
wouldn't have been threatened and had nothing to do with this horrendous act. These were pretender gods who displayed their "godliness"
by destroying rather than creating.

What the emerging humans feared most happened:

Thus, the LORD dispersed them from there all over the
earth, so they had to stop building the city.

That is why its name was called Babel, because it was
there that the LORD made a Babel of the language of
the whole earth, and it was there that the LORD dispersed them all over the earth.

So the Lord scattered them abroad from thence upon
the face of the earth.

How can any compassionate human being feel good about
this? This was a rape of the soul and spirit. Some very creative people
were smashed—and then dumbed down so that they would never do
this again. How can we feel good about a "God" who would do this?

There is nothing spiritual or Godly about this. It is extreme cruelty for no real offense.

The message that the pretender Gods were sending was "don't create". Don't do anything that might set you free. Don't bond together in community and communal spirit. Instead I want you separate and to be strewn all over the earth. Is it possible that the pretender gods actually separated families and sent them to different places? Could the separation of African families in the mid 19th century have been the result of past shock?

This is a horror story that tops anything that Stephen King has written.

## Babel's Modern Impact

This Tower of Babel story is not a minor event that happened long, long ago and is easily forgotten. The impact of Babel is powerful in these millennial times. In the modern workplace and in education we have a mentality that tells us we should not go beyond a certain point.

Often kids in high school classes who "cause trouble" find that it is the only way they can express themselves creatively. When I was a high school teacher, I found that giving "trouble-making" students creative projects and urging them to share what they learned with the class usually solved the problem.

At Grossmont College I had a student who interrupted me incessantly, telling me that my ideas were sexist. In fairness, she did compliment me for using the expression "he or she" in my lectures. Yet she was an arch-feminist who felt oppressed by what I was teaching. I asked her to come to my office and allow her to vent her frustration. She exclaimed how she chose her teachers based on word of mouth from other students she respected. She exclaimed, "Do you know how sick I am of hearing that you and Mr. Burton (a psychology teacher) are God?"

In one of my greatest comebacks I almost lost Peggy: "Peggy, Mr. Burton is not God."

She didn't laugh. In fact, she was offended, but it also loosened her up. I then began suggested ways that she could get creatively involved in the class. She had mentioned some anti-feminist writers who "drove her crazy". I asked her if she had read some of them, and she said that she would not bother. I told her that if she would read these writers, I would give her a half hour of class time to present these ideas and then refute them. Her excitement was immediate. She saw the challenge of understanding "the enemy" by pointing out the flaws in the author's logic.

She came to my office and reported her progress. This was education as it should be, but rarely is. Her talk was brilliant, the students loved it, and Peggy no longer gave me any trouble. True to her integrity, she raised her hand and disagreed with me on issues, but this was never disruptive and the class members could sense the mutual respect.

Another college where I recently taught presented to me some unique students. One, named Bridgett, was constantly in my office complaining that she felt thwarted because she would get things quickly and get bored waiting for the rest of the class to catch up with her.

I knew this to be true because at this school we were obsessed with making our department the champion of the remedial student. Long hours were spent in portfolio readings for the remedial students, but absolutely no time was spent on the transfer level courses — courses students needed to transfer to a four-year college. Our transfer level courses were left in shambles so that we could improve the writing of our remedial level courses.

This is insane — until one begins to consider that this may be fallout from the Tower of Babel event. During meetings, most English students felt that courses like Shakespeare, World Literature, and other literature courses should be scrapped to make way for high school level remedial courses. One teacher vehemently said, "I'm tired of catering to the whims of all these English majors. Let's get rid of these [literature] courses." This is what happened: the literature courses were "torn down" so that high school level remedial courses could take their place.

After the Tower of Babel incident, the builders—the more intelligent of the human species—were dumbed down and scattered all over the earth. The reward for creativity was punishment and a stultifying of the mind's process. In our present American colleges and universities, the main population of students is being dumbed down and being given little opportunity for creative expression. If you want a degree, you must sit in a classroom and listen to a professor who lectures but no longer educates. With the greatest of ironies, higher education in the United States costs more money and results in the same stultification of the mind. Some small businesses are wising up and intentionally avoiding the hiring of college graduates. The reasoning for this is that hiring someone 24 years old with six years of full time work experience is much better than hiring a 24 year-old college graduate with only limited work experience.

Our colleges and universities have become Towers of Babel. I watch every August as excited students start their freshman year. Usually by the middle of their first semester, they realize that what they are experiencing is more about fitting in that grasping knowledge. By the middle of the second semester, most are disillusioned. Most want to learn, but the curriculum is geared to a dumbed down "middle ground", which sinks lower and lower each year.

Imagine an advertisement stating the following:

Come to college. It costs a lot and you won't learn very much, but we need your tuition money to keep going. Besides, if you stay with us for four years, you will raise your level of education to what a fifteen-year-old Japanese student knows.

Babel lives today in the form of extended past shock in our colleges and universities. The dumbing down of students at all levels has been extensive, but one level that should not have crumbled was the American college and university system. However, stringent tenure laws protect the teachers who are incompetent and those who refuse to grasp that our society is changing rapidly. Teachers who are creative and capable of motivating students to great knowledge and skills are "beaten down" by their own colleagues. Those with effective teaching skills have less of a chance of being hired than teachers who say politically correct things during interviews.

In many ways the humans that emerged from the Tower of Babel incident got much farther along than today's college students. These "modern" students are immediately pushed into a narrow paradigm and told to stay there if they want to do well. If a pre-med student gets an insight into a potential cure for cancer, he will usually be brushed off, laughed at or told to wait until he becomes a doctor.

For three years I was advisor for a group of highly motivated students who wanted to explore where constitutional law is being broken, a position in which no other faculty member was interested. Our greatest success was putting on a town meeting and inviting three people to speak on constitutional issues. As soon as we announced who the speakers would be, my faculty mailbox was flooded:

> Why have you brought such people on campus to speak? This shames the school.

> It makes me sick that you are exposing your students to such filth.

> If clear thinking students are there, they will vociferously argue with your chosen speakers. Be aware that it is your obligation to break up any fights.

The meeting was an exciting event and went without incident—other than liberals and conservatives making points and listening to each other, something that rarely happens in the classroom. All three speakers were excellent and stimulated thought. Students from my classes and other's were thrilled:

> I came expecting to be bored, but this was really interesting.

> I learned so much about our constitution, and it was really exciting.

> Why can't we have things like this in our classes?

In any college classroom, the teacher feels that he or she is king. While class is certainly not a democracy, few teachers are even willing to bring in speakers who might contradict their own established viewpoints. Students have told me hundreds of horror stories about what happened when they wrote something that differed from the teacher's opinion. Despite backing their own ideas with solid evidence and research, they still got lower grades because they dared to depart from their teacher's worldview.

I wonder if sometime during the early 1970's a group of educational leaders gathered and said the following:

> We are educating our students too well. They are gathering critical thinking skills and using them against us. They are of one mind and daring to question our authority. Come—let us go and dumb them down so that they might be more easily controlled.

Of course, no one ever did that because that would be ridiculous. However, in *Past Shock* I asked, "If we were not created as slaves, then why, thousands of years later, are we still acting as slaves?" In relation to higher education, I ask, "If these students were not intentionally dumbed down, then how come they are acting and performing as if they have been?"

## Babel and Religion

I strongly believe that very few people explore religions with any depth. Usually the exploration is in the form of classes or Bible studies, which make damn sure that whatever is explored is done within the framework of the religion's tenets. However, religion is doing great harm if it presents itself as the only true religion and suggests that exploration is not necessary. This is more closely aligned with brainwashing than spiritual nourishment. This is best explained in the opening lines of a punk rock song by the Dead Milkmen:

> You got a Methodist coloring book
> And you color really well
> But don't color outside the lines
> Or God will send you to hell

Thousands of years ago in Sumer, a group of pretender gods must have gotten together and said something similar to what was said by the gods after finding out about the Tower of Babel:

> These humans are starting to question the spiritual values we have taught them. If they continue to explore on their own, they may find out that we are pretender gods, and our power to make them worship us will be diminished. Come—let us go down and really kick ass. Let us so browbeat and brainwash them, that they will have no choice but to believe that we are the true gods.

I am frightened by the control that exists today in modern religion. It might have been somewhat understandable when the technologically advanced pretender gods were hovering over humanity, watching their every move. If a group of people did manage to sneak away to an isolated area and begin building a city and a tower, that must have really frightened the pretender gods. This resulted in a spiritual rape so that the humans could be controlled.

While the pretender gods aren't here now, their Ruling Priest Class has survived intact. This "priest class" makes sure that the chains of control are pulled tight:

> If a Protestant and a Catholic marry, the pressure is extremely strong that the children be raised Catholic. Instead of encouraging children to explore on their own about spiritual matters, most parents begin conditioning children immediately about the ideas of their own religion. They feel that this is their duty.

> A teenager who begins to probe ideas different from his parent's faith is usually not encouraged in his exploration. Some parents will claim that he is straying from the path or opening himself to the influence of Satan.

The idea here is "don't investigate, don't be creative, and for heaven's sake don't go building any cities or towers that will upset a god with an extremely limited paradigm." During a visit to the town of Buena Vista, Colorado, I observed that there were multiple Christian bookstores but none that sold general books. I asked where I could find some secular books. "None in this town, praise the Lord," the owner said. Not only was Buena Vista a town of predominantly born again Christians, but it also struck me as being "super white." While the town was originally pronounced "Brey-na Vista," the pronunciation was changed to "Boo-na Vista."

While it is rare to find such an exceptionally oppressive town, some churches and some families more easily follow the "don't let them explore, don't let them build" mentality.

I have heard of pastors accompanying church members to stores to ensure that they buy the right books and avoid buying something interesting, but not along spiritually acceptable lines. This is much like saying, "You can explore all you want as long as you don't leave the house (don't color outside the lines)". Knowing that Adam and Eve were curious people, Jehovah never should have put the Tree of Knowledge in the middle of the Garden. If this was Jehovah's attempt at setting up Adam and Eve, it worked beautifully; Adam and Eve were snapped out of their exploration mode mighty quickly. So were those highly creative people of Babel who built a city and a tower and were then brutally punished.

The true God does not discourage exploration.

## The Eleventh Commandment: Thou Shalt Not Explore

The fallout from the Babel incident is that most humans have little or no desire to explore. In ancient times, humans were building a city and a tower and wanted to share it with the world. There was nothing wrong with this. No one was being hurt. Yet some very insecure pretender gods found this threatening. Thus they created an incident that destroyed the Babylonian's work and caused them to feel guilty about it.

I wonder when people are going to stand up and say, "Jehovah, at the Tower of Babel, you went too far." However, we have been brainwashed into thinking that it was humanity who went too far. A phrase in Genesis 11: 4 suggests some mild arrogance on the part of the Babylonians, but if the emerging humans needed some humility, Jehovah's reaction was like dropping a bomb on a house to get rid of termites. The punishment far exceeded the "crime."

How does that impact us today?

In the workplace obedience is stressed much more than creativity. A friend of mine, Alex, worked at a large defense contracting company. After being with the company for eight years, he worked on a plan to improve the efficiency of his department. He worked on his proposal for three weeks, and then a very excited Alex asked for time to present his proposal.

Most people were thrilled with his ideas; more teamwork and less useless tasks would greatly increase morale. However, Alex's three bosses didn't take kindly to his proposal. During a meeting in one of their offices, Alex was read the riot act.

> Do you know what you're doing? You're trying to undermine our authority. Do you realize the chaos that something like this would create? [This translates into, "Do you know how much less power we will have over our workers?"] We hired you to follow orders and do what you're told. And this is what we are telling you to do: forget this scheme; don't even mention it again. Otherwise you can look for work elsewhere.

Alex was making $87,500 a year as a mid-manager. In a Hollywood movie he would have said, "I quit" and after a few discouraging searches would have landed a job with another employer. However, in the real world, Alex didn't have a chance. He stifled his creative impulses and did what he was told.

While some employers are starting to adopt a much more creative form of leadership, most still make the workplace a non-inventive environment. New ideas must be discussed to death and are usually defeated by the "this is the way we've always done it" gang. Most people in the workplace don't come up with new ideas because they are not heeded. They learn quickly to stifle themselves and not "rock the boat."

This was certainly the message given after the destruction of the Tower of Babel: if you get creative and come up with things on your own, we're going to get mean.

More than likely this tower and city would have been a significant advancement for humanity. What makes the story so tragic is that these humans wanted to share it with others, and there was a genuine level of excitement about what they were doing. If they wanted to get credit for that it and "make a name for themselves," so what!

Yet memories linger at deep levels—perhaps at the cellular level. In Rollo May's *The Courage to Create,* it talks about the fear people have of creating. Some experience anxiety when they approach something creatively. May mentions that creativity is associated with destruction. People who create know that they are going to have to destroy on some level if they are going to bring something new into the world.

Perhaps we can go a little bit further and explore the idea that creativity might be associated with destruction because, at humanity's most creative moment, their tower, city, language, and clarity of mind were destroyed.

When I announced to my parents that I wanted to leave teaching and write full-time, I got looks as though I had just told them that I wanted to round up a group of teenage girls and lure them into prostitution. Writing is, for the most part, a very creative act. One creates something out of nothing and enjoys the process. It becomes even more fun if a lot of people read your created book. However, my parents and so many others viewed writing as a dead-end career.

The same is true with people who want to be artists or sculptors. They may look mighty in a film, but parents who have more "acceptable" ideas for their children's careers and would like them to "make something of themselves" frown upon artistic careers. (Making something of yourself sounds very creative until one realizes that what you make of yourself usually must fit within an extremely narrow paradigm of those who are trying to control you.)

Thanks to the events of Babel, the pressure is to avoid being creative rather than embrace it.

During my years in seminary, I found this out the hard way. In my contemporary theology class, I was required to write a paper on original sin. The idea excited me, and I started reading different theologians views on original sin. This was a very exciting project, and even the laborious task of synthesizing these different theologians was an act of creativity that increased my own perception of the idea of original sin.

The fact that the project was an act of creativity was my problem. My excitement about blazing new trails was not shared by my professor. He gave the 15-page paper a C—the lowest grade that is usually given in graduate school.

Despondent, I went home and talked with my wife. She remembered that while I was getting my Master's Degree at the University of Pittsburgh, I had told her about an impossible course during my first graduate degree. Statistical analysis was extremely difficult for me, and to save my sanity, I decided that I would just go for a C. My wife Mary had also suggested that I take it easy and let this be my C course. This struck me as a good idea—after all, she was putting me through school and we needed to spend more time together.

For the next assigned paper, I just relaxed. The requirement was 5-15 pages and I did 3 1/2. This time I had no creativity. I didn't even do any synthesis or have an original thought. I simply quoted one person and then put in the quote of another person and then had two or three sentences of banal commentary. This was a test to see if I could indeed do work of such poor quality and still maintain a C. As the papers were being turned back, I muttered a quick prayer: "Come on, God. Just let it be a C."

When I got the paper back, I went into shock. In the upper right hand corner was an A-. The accompanying note rocked me even more:

> Mr. Barranger, it pains me greatly that I couldn't give you a solid A for this paper. This is excellent work. However, I had to drop you to an A-.

It was then that I remembered that once I finished typing the paper, I hadn't even proofread it.

What's the point of this personal story? What does it have to do with the Tower of Babel?

The point for me was that creativity in this environment got me in trouble. The point for others is that creativity is greatly discouraged for a lot of people in work, family, church, or community. Most likely this discouragement came from events like the Garden of Eden and the Tower of Babel.

While people in all areas of life give lip service to creativity and creative people, these same people have a continuous loop tape playing in their heads:

Remember what happened when you got creative at Babel.

Remember what happened when you explored rather than followed orders in Eden.

We created you. Don't you try to create anything.

Our programmers are gone, but the programming remains intact. The human race is a race of obeyers rather than creators. We have a hierarchy that has a chain of command going from the top down. When Scandinavian Airlines was losing money, a creative CEO turned the company upside down and asked ticket sellers and baggage people to make suggestions. The morale of the Airline increased to such a point that people at the low end of the scale felt important, and people at the top felt they were getting valuable information. The following year Scandinavian Airlines was the only airline that made a profit.

Creativity and innovation work when a sense of community and bonding become more important than everyone simply following orders from above. If this had happened at Babel, we might be an entirely different race. However, our pretender gods were dreadfully insecure. They couldn't allow humanity to move to a self-sufficient and spiritually free way of life.

According to Egyptian writings, a group of rebels existed in the ranks of the pretender gods. They were referred to as The Brotherhood of the Serpent. The members of this group were not evil. Instead they had compassion for their human creations and knew that they were spiritual beings. They wanted to teach humans how to break free spiritually. While this group was referred to very briefly as the serpent in the Garden of Eden, Sumerian and Egyptian texts refer to pretender gods who were sick of what was happening to the newly created human race.

In the Sumerian literature, particularly the *Atra-hasis* and the *Enuma Elish,* two main gods oversee the humans rather than one.

Enlil is mean and sees the humans only as slaves. When he had knowledge of a coming flood, he told no humans and "hovered above" as the human race was drowning. In contrast, Enki, as the creator of humanity, had more compassion for his charges. He—or someone very close to him—was most likely the serpent in the Garden of Eden. He also was the one who warned Utnapishtam that a flood was coming and to build an ark. In the Sumerian version, evidently more than seven people were saved.

Enki taught language, agriculture, and mathematics to the new humans. Much of the time he treated them with respect. However, they were still expected to be worker/slaves.

The *Atra-hasis* tells of Enki and Enlil inside a big flying machine watching humans being destroyed by the flood. Enlil, in an uncharacteristic moment, wept... just a little. Sensing compassion, Enki mentioned that he had saved some of the humans. Enki judged wrong about the compassion, because Enlil flew into a rage and punished Enki.

All of this leads up to what happened to the Brotherhood of the Serpent and the positive impact it had on the emerging human race. What if some members of the Brotherhood took a large group of humans and helped them build a tower and a city? What if this was a secret experiment in a far off place with increasingly intelligent humans? This is speculation, but it is worth exploring.

As soon as the efforts of the Brotherhood were discovered, the Enlil/Jehovah group[1] realized that they had to come down hard on the humans—so hard that the efforts of the Brotherhood would be futile. The scattering of these humans all over the earth and dumbing them down by confounding their language could have been the means to serve an end. The means were brutal but the end result of achieving obedience and following orders was restored. The slaves were no longer creative and resourceful, and this was just fine with the pretender gods.

The Bad Religion song "Skyscraper" mentioned in *Past Shock* effectively conveys the horror of the time of Babel. This is a punk rock song speaking of the joy of building a "tower for the world. And climb so that we can reach anything we propose."

The optimism of this song is initially infectious. The second verse names the destroyer as a "spoiled little baby [who] can't come out and play."

The lyrics of the final verse express the horror:

> Well madness reigned and paradise drowned.
> When Babel's walls came crashing down
> Now the echoes roar, the story lived
> That was hardly understood, and never any
> good.

This song is a wake up call to people who think that it is all right to dumb people down, confound their language, and scatter them around the world.

The song and the Tower of Babel story—despite only occupying eight verses in the Old Testament—is a wake up call to people who suppress their creativity and choose instead to "go along to get along." This began thousands of years ago because of pretender gods who were everywhere, intruding into and creating spiritual terrorism with the emerging human race.

Because we were very impressionable, and were punished severely, we figured that we must have done something wrong.

But we didn't do anything wrong. That's just what the pretender gods said, and they backed it with utter destruction. Today, the pretender gods are gone, leaving us to fend for ourselves. We have the choice to be more creative, more resourceful, and more in charge of our destinies. However, thanks to moments in the past that never should have happened, many quiver in the dark, looking for a pretender god replacement to give them a command to obey.

The story is lived, now the echoes roar and little of it is understood. The more we understand it, the more we can break free of Babel's curse and move toward being highly creative human beings once again.

It is a noble goal... with no gods to interfere.

NOTES TO CHAPTER TWO

1. Many writing about Sumerian society and its relation to society feel that Jehovah and Enlil were the same god.

*Chapter Three*

# The Ascending Tyrants:
# Remnants of the Ruling Priest Class

Since humanity has learned language skills, a force has arisen to use language as a means to enslave and tyrannize people. In ancient Egypt and Israel, and even further back in ancient Sumer, the Ruling Priest Class was a group with great powers. Not only did these priests determine theological law, they also determined reality. This select group of people determined laws and ruled on what could be believed and what couldn't.

These priests emerged after the pretender gods left earth—or died off. They rushed in to fill the vacuum left by these ancient beings who dared to call themselves gods. Once these "gods" departed, a power struggle began that resulted in a group of self-appointed priests filling in for the ancient gods. These ruling priests maintained the same oppressive power as the "gods" who preceded them.

The Ruling Priest Class did not die out. Like the mythological god Proteus, it has simply shape-shifted into other forms of spiritual tyranny and has requested or demanded spiritual slavery in the name of God, enlightenment, transformation, or even health. The variety of ways this remnant of the Ruling Priest Class rules is legion.

In our ancient past, if a group of priests determined that a mighty temple was going to be built, this was ordained and fulfilled. If a warlord such as Jehovah decided that a city or village was to be destroyed, that was Holy Writ. Democracy and free will were not yet part of the human experience. If Krishna desired that Arjuna lead Arjuna's forces against a Krishna-declared enemy, not even Arjuna's desire for a peaceful settlement had any relevance.

During the time of Jesus, Ruling Priest Class groups like the Pharisees, the Sadducees, and the Sanhedrin were collections of people who had such power that they were able to execute the alleged son of God. Not even Jesus could escape their will.

Centuries later, another Ruling Priest Class informs us that this was all a part of God's plan, that these Ruling Priest Class characters were merely playing a part in a cosmic drama orchestrated by none other than God "himself."

Thanks to the modern remnants of the Ruling Priest Class, people are discouraged from wondering why God didn't just forgive the human race for its alleged accumulation of sins. Why put forth this cosmic drama where Jesus is subjected to brutal torture and extreme pain on the cross so that he can bear the sins of the world? Why institute this barbaric practice when God could have been so much gentler in "His" plan of salvation? The fact that a very high percentage of Christians believe that this was a wonderful act points out how effective the Ruling Priest Class' conditioning was.

It continues today with the remnants of the Ruling Priest Class.

During the Spanish Inquisition, the remnants of the Ruling Priest Class ruled with great power. Dare to have the wrong beliefs and you could be roasting at the stake or languishing in a damp, cold prison praying that pneumonia would quickly end your life.

Equally absurd, for those daring to think that this was simply a Roman Catholic problem, were the terrifying exploits of the Protestant Puritan ministers at the turn of the seventeenth century who determined what witchcraft was, who was a witch, and how these "witches" would have to repent. In Europe the Spanish Inquisition represented the Ruling Priest Class's attack primarily on men, but also on women who were accused of being "witches" not only in Spain, but throughout Europe. When the insanity spread to the New World and the Salem witch trials, the brunt of the insanity was inflicted upon women.

Thank God that we are finally past this insanity. Right?

Wrong.

While no one is burned at the stake for being a heretic or a witch now, that does not mean that the Ruling Priest Class has ceased to function. Remnants of that Ruling Priest Class are still in power, but they have shifted uniforms. Yesterday's Grand Inquisitor may be today's head of the Moral Majority. The seventeenth century bishop who determined who was a witch and who wasn't may now be today's head of the those factions of the American Medical Association who are trying to stamp out alternative medicine. Yesterday's Jonathan Edwards revival preacher who inflicted terror in his congregations by graphically describing the horrors of hell may be today's malfunctioning messiah leading a new age group in a manner that controls rather than liberates.

Today's Ruling Priest Class is no longer limited to priests, ministers, and rabbis. It now includes doctors, chiropractors, psychologists, psychiatrists, and far eastern gurus from halfway around the world, *as well as some priests, ministers and rabbis.*

To claim that all—or even a majority—of men (and women) of the cloth are part of the Ruling Priest Class would be neither accurate nor fair. Despite the fact that they embrace the oppressive theology born of the Ruling Priest Class, the majority of ministers, priests, and rabbis are good people who are unfortunately operating within a bad system. While the majority of them genuinely want to contribute to their members' well-being and spiritual growth, they are unfortunately operating from a paradigm that portrays God more as a tyrant than a liberator.

However, the concept of the Ruling Priest Class in the twenty-first century is no longer limited to people of the cloth. Our version of spiritual tyranny allows for some doctors to assume the role of twisted god rather than healer. On an equal footing is the chiropractor who is no longer content simply to adjust spines; he or she must now adjust attitudes, eating habits, and life styles. A good number of doctors are not spiritual tyrants. The same can be said about chiropractors. Yet, both groups have so much power over a person's life that those possessing a messiah complex can do great harm to their patients.

Laurie was a victim of both a doctor and a chiropractor. She had a back problem so first went to an osteopath who prescribed drugs with devastating side effects. With one of the drugs a severe rash broke out on both her arms and legs. Instead of the doctor being sympathetic, he launched into his "doctor as God" routine:

> Laurie, your back problem is mainly the result
> of stress. You've got to quit your job and find
> less stressful work. Do that and you will find
> that your back problem will take care of itself.

Laurie was a first year teacher in her mid-thirties. Any teacher's first year is highly stressful and in knowing this can be dealt with, but Laurie almost quit her job on her doctor's recommendation. However, her principal and other teachers felt she had the makings of a great teacher. They told her that the second year is much easier. This helped Laurie remain in teaching, but at the time did nothing for her back pain.

A friend recommended a "terrific chiropractor," Doctor Len. What neither Laurie or this friend realized was that Dr. Len's ego was rapidly inflating because of his success. He went from just healing people to telling them what to do with their lives. He was good at adjusting backs, and in this area he provided Laurie some relief.

However, he told Laurie that she must change her diet completely. In addition he had herbs, vitamins, and other products that he claimed would help her with her back pain. Laurie related to me a "Dr. Len haranguing" that I still find hard to believe:

> I can't believe you are still eating lettuce. Do
> you know how toxic lettuce is? You are poi-
> soning yourself, and even worse you are undo-
> ing all the work that we've been doing. Do
> you know what happens when all those toxins
> from the lettuce go into your vertebrate?
> That's right—pain.

Surprisingly, Dr. Len did not recommend exercise. That suggestion came from a friend. Laurie joined a gym, and received free
guidance with exercises that would strengthen her back. That is what
finally reduced her back pain.

To be fair, Dr. Len is not a typical chiropractor.

Another area that is quite frightening from the Ruling Priest
Class remnant is the status of psychologists and psychiatrists. Both of
these sciences are barely a century old. Yet too many within the mental health ranks actually see themselves more as priests than healers.

## A Ruling Sex Priestess

A few months ago, I was visiting a friend in Los Angeles. He
was always current on what guru was worthy of his time. Erica was
David's latest. She was a sex therapist who was making the rounds of
Whole Life Expos and Humanistic Psychology conferences. Her
views, if they weren't so comical, would be at least oppressive.

I went with David to a Saturday night meeting. Erica was
dressed in a skintight leotard outfit that accentuated every luscious
curve of her 42-year-old body. If she had just kept her mouth shut, the
sexual attraction might have continued. However, within three minutes
of her spouting her sex therapy drivel, I had experienced the verbal
equivalent of a cold shower.

Here are some samples of her sexual liberation in the name of oppression talk:

> Don't tell me that you're free. You have been
> very badly conditioned about sex. You have so
> many hang-ups playing around in your pathet-
> ically programmed little brains that you
> wouldn't know a free thought if it bit you in
> the ass. If you're not having sex at least once
> a day, you're not mentally healthy.

Considering my sparse sex life at the time, I figured that I must have been close to borderline psychosis. She continued with her overly explicit and offensive tirade:

> I can't believe what the f***ing Christian
> church has done to us. They have not only
> made sex evil, but they have even made think-
> ing about sex evil. Come on, Jesus. Come on,
> Paul. Get a life!

> God didn't give us all this sexual energy and
> capacity to shut it off. You want to know what
> I call the shutting off of this sexual energy?
> Sin. That's right, sin. S... I... N.... Do you
> know how many Bible banging ministers are
> praying for me right now? You know what I
> say to those so-called people of God? F***
> your wife a few times more each day and you
> wouldn't worry about all this shit.

Despite religion's shortcomings, it hit me that sex was somehow not the answer. One first time visitor—who was not aware that the audience was stacked with Erica's disciples—complained bitterly about Erica's being one-sided. She suggested that something could be gained from celibacy. At this point Erica went into her Ruling Priest Class mode:

> Lady, I sure hope you wake up. Whatever is
> holding you back is preventing you from
> experiencing the fullness of life.

Applause broke out from about 80% of the people in the room. I was not one of the ones applauding. I was horrified:

> You aren't going to understand this until you
> let go of all your Puritanical conditioning. You
> think you are so spiritual for staying away
> from sex. Lady, that thing between your legs
> was made for more than peeing.

More applause. I turned and asked David how this woman was different from a narrow-minded fundamentalist minister who was railing out against what he considered to be illicit sex. I watched as this poor woman continued to be whipped by the zealous Erica. She picked up on the crowd's energy and used it to destroy the woman who did nothing more wrong than having an opinion that went against one of the current remnants of the Ruling Slave Class.

I have what some among my friends refer to as a severe problem. When I see someone being attacked by a rabid member of the Ruling Priest Class, I immediately want to be their ally. I don't want them to stand alone. I stood up waving my hand yearning to speak. Erica acknowledged me and encouraged me to share what I was feeling. What follows was a total put on. However, it had more truth than Erica's "righteous" ramblings:

> Ah, I know what she's talking about. But I'm
> a little different. I really get off on Beethoven.
> I put on Beethoven's Ninth Symphony, and I
> have such ecstasy that I'm not going to ruin it
> with sex.

The room went silent, and a group of forty people just stared at me, the biggest stare coming from David. I could tell from his look that he wanted to make doggone sure that no one knew that I had come with him.

> You know that last movement when the chorus comes in? It's so sublime. It's almost like Beethoven is penning his own orgasm as he was writing this. You know he was deaf when he wrote this symphony, yet he experienced more ecstasy writing this symphony than most people experience rolling in the hay.

Erica gave me such a look that I got the impression that, at the time, she wished that *she* was deaf. I looked around the room and could see what most people felt about this sublime description I was giving. It had no place in a room of people who wanted to get so in touch with their bodies that they would allow a certain organ of their body to rule everything else.

What frightened me the most was the fact that only a few people could sense that I was putting Erica on.

The only ally I had was the "errant" woman who dared speak on behalf of celibacy.

She walked up to me after the meeting, and I wondered if this couldn't be the beginning of some friendship... until she asked, "Is Beethoven really that good?"

**The Secular Priest Class**

The Ruling Priest Class is a nomenclature for people who are in positions to manipulate people in the name of helping them. This could be a Tibetan monk who is more into controlling people than he is into liberating them. It could be a therapist who subjects her clients to all the latest new age therapies, but never stays with one long enough to determine its effectiveness. This could also be a doctor who has no interest in what the patient's needs are but instead inflicts "his particular thing" onto most of them.

This happened in a rural town in Washington state. No matter what ailment a person came to the doctor with, the doctor almost always prescribed Prozac. The doctor became both a spiritual zealot and a medical tyrant. His zeal for the drug Prozac exceeded his medical wisdom. True, he was a doctor with a mission, and in his mind he was healing hundreds of people. By the time a 1995 program about this town and doctor aired on a television magazine show, he had 72 of his patients on Prozac.

Excuse the pun, but that's depressing.

Why is it depressing? Consider that Prozac may be good for some of the people. However, this doctor is very much like a person who has had a religious conversion experience. He wanted everyone to experience what he had. While no one knows for sure exactly what each and every one of those peoples' ailments were, the fact that most of them get Prozac as the answer is a form of spiritual and medical tyranny. The doctor's zeal had blinded him to the fact that depression is often a symptom of deeper medical problems.

This doctor meant well; but that does not mean that he did well.

## Never Have So Few—the Fruits of the Misguided Clergyman

Of course, the most popular stereotype of the spiritual tyrant is the misguided clergyman. By their own admission, most of them are frightened by the power that they have over people. Put another way, these people of the cloth are frightened by the power that members of their congregation are willing to surrender to them. Those with these concerns usually are not spiritual tyrants. However, while these spiritual leaders mean well, they are espousing a doctrine that is laced with spiritual tyranny.

In my book *Knowing When to Quit,* I asked the following question:

> Why do good people end up in bad situations?

For this book I would like to pose a new question:

> Why are well-meaning spiritual leaders espousing such bad doctrine?

Put another way, the question would come out in the form of a paradox:

> Why do spiritual leaders who want to liberate people do such a good job of keeping them spiritually enslaved?

## Well-Meaning People Creating Spiritual Slavery in the Name of God

Two facts must be emphasized again. First, some religious and/or spiritual leaders do consciously and unconsciously utilize spiritually tyrannical methods to manipulate members of their congregations. Second, nowhere near the majority of pastors, priests, or rabbis consciously attempt to manipulate people in a bad way. Unfortunately, most carry the belief-baggage carried down culturally from past spiritual tyranny into their practices.

The most compassionate Jewish rabbi still carries the tradition of a psychologically perverse Jehovah as part of his work. Rarely will the rabbi challenge the absurd concept of animal sacrifices or question why Jehovah demanded an almost pathological obedience from the emerging Israelite tribes.

The fact that a whole family can be killed because one family member withheld two pieces of gold during the sack of Jericho is neither questioned nor explored. Nor is having a man stoned to death because he dared to pick up a stick on the Sabbath. Because they are part of the sacred tradition or couched within the safe realms of Holy Scripture, they become part of a heritage that allows both present and past tyranny. Jehovah was a tyrant; therefore, spiritual tyranny begins at the top and rolls downhill.

The dedicated Catholic priest may have compassion and a genuine dedication to helping people live a better life with the help of God. Yet he is part of religious tradition that murdered millions of people simply because they possessed the "wrong" beliefs. He is part of the faith that burned the Aztec holy books, and—according to some Native American sources—took the Mayan holy books from the Mayan people and shipped them back to the Old World where they now sit in the Vatican basement. Hidden from public scrutiny are books from the *Dead Sea Scrolls*, which show the Apostle Paul as a potential deceiver and destroyer of the faith instead of in a more favorable light. No matter how well intentioned the priest, the heritage from which he comes is laced with spiritual tyranny.

The well-meaning Protestant minister may be a friend to someone in need and a rock of faith to lean on in many situations. However, that rock can be slippery because it comes as a packaged deal, which contains the belief that Jesus was the son of God, that God actually would send non-believers to hell, and that humans by nature are sinful creatures who need God's redemption. This is not a spiritually healthy foundation from which to experience spiritual freedom. The threads of spiritual tyranny are so subtly weaved into the Protestant experience that they no longer look oppressive. All you have to do is have the spiritually correct beliefs and thou shalt be accepted into the fold. While this is rarely directly stated, it is almost always expected to be part of the spiritual experience.

The rabbi, the priest, and the pastor have all done acts that nourish both the heart and the spirit. However, because all three operate on a foundation and history of spiritual tyranny, the potential for spiritual harm is always there—even with the most well meaning of spiritual leaders.

Steve and Alice Marshall experienced a devastating example of spiritual tyranny from a well meaning Protestant minister. Steve and Alice both worshipped at a suburban Chicago church. The minister did indeed love children, and it was obvious that he enjoyed being around them. He loved children so much that his pastoral counseling sessions with childless couples would increasingly focus upon the idea of being fruitful and multiplying.

Steve and Alice had decided that they did not want to have children. Their pastor, Reverend Allworth, however, would have none of it. He advised every childless couple to have children as soon as possible after marriage. In Reverend Allworth's highly limited paradigm, a wait of two years is permissible... as long as the wife is pregnant in that two-year period. According to Reverend Allworth, both people working and having careers of their own was simply not in God's plan. After three and a half years of Alice's not even becoming pregnant, the hyper-concerned reverend began applying the spiritual pressure:

> I know that you both have careers that are fulfilling and seemingly add meaning to your lives, but you are avoiding God's plan. Alice, God created you to be a vehicle for new souls coming into the world. You were created to be a mother, not a career woman. I know that the way of the world is for women to do their own thing and avoid their duties to be mothers. However, this is wrong, and you are wrong to be avoiding your sacred duty to bring children into the world. God is leading me to tell you to sow the seeds now for the raising of a family. Do God's will. Our own wills will only bring us unhappiness. Only through fulfilling God's plan will both of you find the happiness that you so much deserve.

Steve and Alice didn't feel unhappy at all. They were enjoying their lives and each found their work fulfilling. However, Reverend Alworth exercised his spiritual tyranny when he claimed that this was selfish.

The ever "helpful" Reverend Allworth even scheduled a meeting with an adoption agency so that their child-filled future could begin as soon as possible. It was then that Steve and Alice owned up to the fact that they had been using birth control. This "revelation" caused the normally docile Allworth to soar into indignant rage:

> How do you think the Lord feels right now?
> You have lied to me and the Lord. Can you
> imagine the hurt, the sadness that God must
> feel knowing that you are deceiving Him?

The problem was that Reverend Allworth somehow got his role and God's mixed up. If God is omniscient, He already was aware of Steve and Alice's situation and the fact that they were actually getting help in preventing conception. The reverend's speech and tone gave the impression that God was just finding out, much in the same manner as the pastor. Since no form of birth control is perfect, God could have made sure that Alice got pregnant despite their efforts.

The fact is that God probably didn't care one way or the other whether or not Alice got pregnant.

The sad thing is that spiritual tyranny is such a part of the pastor/congregation experience that like so many other people, it never occurred to Steve and Alice to say, "Look, this is none of your business; just drop it," nor "I think I'll deal directly with God on this one, and I'd really appreciate it if you would not interfere."

Reverend Allworth had such an impact on this young couple that they actually began to feel that they were selfish for wanting to have lives of their own—without (at least at this point) the responsibility of having to raise children. The reverend's unfortunate advice gnawed at Steve and Alice. After all, he was a man of God. He must be right.

He wasn't.

He had no business telling this young couple how to live their lives. This would be manipulative enough. However, he couched this advice with the fallacious appeal to the authority. This is one of the lowest forms of spiritual tyranny.

Harry and Laurie Anderson, another married couple, ran into the same problem with their parish priest. Laurie, a devout Catholic from early childhood, was having problems with oral sex being a part of their sexual experience. He enjoyed it immensely, and so did she. However, she genuinely believed that there must be something wrong with it. She worked up the courage to talk about it with her priest. He immediately went into a state of indignant shock:

> You must stop this immediately. The pleasure of sex was meant to be aligned only with the creation of life. No life has a chance of being created when you are doing that as part of your sexual experience.

Laurie told me that Father Wright had such a look of disgust on his face, that she thought this might be appropriate for sado-masochistic sex or ultra-kinky goings-on that are practiced only in the fringes of the sexual experience. "Father Wright just stopped breathing," Laurie said. "I wasn't talking about walking on my husband's chest with high heels or walking him around with a doggie collar. This is just oral sex, for Christ's sake!"

Laurie mentioned as tactfully as possible that she didn't agree with the priest. She quickly decided that what they did in their bedroom was their own business.

Father Wright disagreed. "Your mortal soul is in danger," he stated.

## Why the Ruling Priest Class Remnant Survives

During the time following our creation as a slave race, we were very curious and demanded to know why we should believe what we were told to. We also rebelled against the menial work that we did for the pretender gods. In these ancient times, many refused to fight wars for these gods. As developed more deeply in *Past Shock,* religion was created as a way to condition and control these rebellious humans.

Through genetic manipulation and religious conditioning these humans eventually became an obeying mass of humanity. Blind obedience was rewarded. Creativity and spiritual exploration were stifled.

This religious conditioning was so effective that humans willingly conditioned themselves long after the pretender gods left. This conditioning continues today in churches and synagogues. While the conditioning was highly tyrannical and stultifying to spiritual and personal freedom, a majority of people reading this in the United States would find this claim (of continued conditioning by us) to be more offensive than the heinous act of the pretender gods' conditioning.

This book's ideas are not blasphemous. The brutal acts of the pretender gods were blasphemous. An increasing minority of people is finally beginning to realize that. However, the majority wants a religion that is like a TV dinner—pre-packed with little toil required.

The Ruling Priest Class remnant remains because people allow these spiritual tyrants to tell them what to believe. In many cases, they even allow them to tell them what to do.

It is so easy to embrace the religion that one is brought up with. Yet increasing numbers are breaking away from their parents' religion. Sadly, too many of these spiritual explorers end up in circumstances that are equally tyrannical, such as the secular and new age version of the spiritual tyrant. In one of the greatest ironies in the human experience, a person will leave his or her church and link up with a new age group, a misguided therapist, or one of the flourishing new age therapies that could be even more tyrannical than the religion they left.

Many people want to be told what to do. They do not yet have the skills, mindset or freedom to spiritually explore on their own. They carry around the misguided concept that there must be one true religion, and they are looking for it.

Freeing themselves of sin, they embrace the equally oppressive concept of karma.

Sick of the Christian hymns, they now have a guru who is telling them to chant Sanskrit mantras—sometimes hundreds of times a day.

Breaking free of a bullying priest, they are now allowing themselves to be led by therapists on talk radio, or any other replacement authority.

The ancient conditioning is there. The song is over but the melody lingers on. Hitler and his army were destroyed more than sixty years ago, but an increasing number of self-proclaimed Nazis is growing in both Europe and America. The mindset of following anything that appears strong is still there. Most people do not want to figure it out for themselves. They simply want someone else to figure it out for them.

Some move onto a form of spiritual terrorism where they are obsessed with the idea that others must have the same experience or share the same beliefs that they have.

# *Chapter Four*

# Spiritual Terrorism

## Frightening people into believing

Terrorism is an emotionally loaded word. When the word comes up in a conversation, most people think of the IRA blowing up a pub in London, the 9-11 tragedy, or some radical Islamic Fundamentalist group causing an airplane to explode over Scotland. This is physical terrorism that has the goal of killing people—or at least spreading terror with the threat of explosions or assassinations.

Physical terrorism is not what will be discussed in this chapter. This book is more concerned about a terrorism that happens in the name of God, transformation, enlightenment, or the attempt to force one's spiritual views on another. This is an emotional, mental form of spiritual terrorism which future history might never fully understand. Done under the aegis of religion, new age philosophy, or radical therapy, people look the other way or simply fail to consider the harm of spiritual terrorism.

## What exactly is Spiritual Terrorism?

Spiritual terrorism occurs when a person or a people feel that they have the truth and use intrusive and extremely manipulative tactics to bring others to their level of "truth". One is a spiritual terrorist when he has been told by another person that she is not interested in the religion, spiritual experience, radical theory, or guru's teachings, but the zealot continues to intrude upon the person's spiritual freedom by harassment, attempts to control, or a variation of continual manipulative devices.

An acquaintance of mine, Phil, experienced the ultimate spiritual terrorism when he took his new girlfriend, Tammy, home to meet his parents. Being a gentleman, Phil offered to go to church with her since she never missed church and could not bear to do so. Phil's relatives allowed her to call the local Mormon church to get the correct time for the service, so all the arrangements were made. While Phil waited in the car, Tammy said she forgot something and went back inside. She slipped into a side room and phoned them again. She did not know that Phil's sister was in earshot and overheard Tammy's plan. She asked that a team be ready to work on Phil after the service.

After the service, Phil was love bombed. Appearing to be as spontaneous as possible, a number of people came up and talked to him and Tammy. Despite the fact that this was all set up, the people pretended that there was no previous conversation with Tammy, no plan for an "ambush," and that they were simply running into them coincidentally. (In most circles this would be considered to be lying.)

Extending the lie, they asked Phil and Tammy if they were Latter Day Saints. Tammy said that she was and Phil stated that he was not.

What a "wonderful" charade.

"Would you like to learn more about our faith?" a number of people asked Phil.

Before he could answer, three members of the group suggested that they go inside where it was warm and talk. Once inside the manipulation began. People explained how becoming a Latter Day Saint had brought so much happiness in their lives. Phil for the first time looked at each of the twelve people and concluded that they didn't look that happy.

He mentioned to Tammy that he wanted to get back home, but Tammy had conversion on her mind. She had found the perfect man except for one fatal flaw: he wasn't of the right faith, and she was bound and determined that this was going to happen as quickly as possible.

According to Phil, one girl was particularly obnoxious. She said, "You have no idea how happy you'll be once you join this church. The difference it made in my life is something indescribable. The only way you can have this is to embrace the true faith. If you don't do that you are stuck with your misery."

Phil simply replied that he didn't have any misery. The person he thought was miserable was this pathetic woman who looked anything but happy.

The group upped the ante of their pressure by urging him to convert to the faith. What a joyful day it would be if he did it right now. This was their last shot because in just a few hours Phil and Tammy would be flying back to the west coast. Because each member most likely knew this, each one turned on the pressure. One man's pressure tactics not only reflected spiritual terrorism but were also pathetic:

"Phil, if we let you out of here we're failing you and we're failing Jesus Christ. We can't in all conscience let you go."

In this group's defense they did not tie Phil to the chair or in any way try to physically restrain him. However, the tears flowing down Tammy's eyes were an added pressure as the man continued speaking:

"How do you think all of us would feel if we let you walk out that door? For all we know we could be letting you walk into hell. Would we be good people if we let you do that? You don't have the wisdom to make these decisions for yourself. God has led us to do all in our power to help you make this the most important decision in your life."

Twenty-four eyes were upon him, and could feel the pressure. Tammy stepped up the pressure by making her crying audible—something that continued on the plane ride back home. However, he held his ground and told these people that his beliefs were adequate for his life. He was forced to become emphatic in stating that he wasn't interested. He actually had to push his way past people as Tammy was trying to pull him back. This group would provide acceptance only if he moved toward their established paradigm.

He didn't. Only after returning to his relative's house was he informed of the overheard phone conversation, with Tammy calling the church and telling them to get a team together. Evidently this is an established procedure for recruitment and is well rehearsed. When they got back to Los Angeles, he cut off his relationship with Tammy immediately.

When one tries to persuade a person that his or her religion is the one true religion, that is pathetic, but it isn't spiritual terrorism. When one keeps pushing despite the lack of interest of the other party, then that is moving toward spiritual terrorism. However, when one pulls out all the stops by attempting to bring the fear of hell into the equation, then we have spiritual terrorism. We also have spiritual terrorism when sincerity spills over into zealousness and people are pressured rather than persuaded. When this pressure moves into bullying, the level of spiritual terrorism increases

## Spiritual Terrorism from the Space Brothers

I have had a great interest in UFOs and its related areas like alien abductions since February of 1980. On February 8, I accompanied an operative of the CIA as he investigated UFOs for the agency. (I found it amazing that the U.S. government takes a very strong stance that there is no such thing as UFOs and then pays CIA operatives to investigate them. If UFOs don't exist, isn't this a waste of taxpayers' money?) What I saw and experienced on that day changed my life and smashed my well-established paradigm. This event increased my interest in UFOs significantly.

During a UFO conference just outside of San Diego with about 50 people, a UFO-inspired reverend was channeling space aliens who were allegedly hovering around our planet ready to give us spiritual guidance. What came forth in this channeling session was nothing short of ugly—an attempt to terrorize people into waking up and "doing the right thing":

"You have poisoned your planet and you have poisoned your souls. You are the lowest creatures in this universe, and without our help you will all perish. Your thoughts are evil and you act on this evil and destroy your own souls. You will pay for this with the Earth changes that are coming in the next two years. [This was happening in August of 1981.] There will be horrors and you will be screaming for mercy. But there will be no mercy, because you are vile creatures."

This was not a fundamentalist Christian minister wreaking the terror of God on his flock. The was the leader of a ministry whose chief goal was to prepare the way for the alien saviors who would save egregious humans from their sinful ways.

Something amazing happened. Both another person and I right on the exact same beat yelled, "Stop!" We both looked at each other, amazed at the timing.

The reverend asked both of us why he should stop. The other person said, "Because what you are saying just isn't healthy." The reverend claimed that this alien entity was "the Christ" (a pathetic appeal to authority if I had ever heard one). I said, "The Christ would never address people like that. The Christ is not about humiliation. This is not the Christ."

Then something really scary happened. A big woman turned to me and snapped, "Who do you think you are stopping the voice of God?" Others chimed in that we were both out of line and should have better manners. However, the channeler could not get himself in the mood to channel again, and that made at least 80% of the audience angry with us. We were persona non grata. Not one person came up and thanked either of us for stopping this spiritual terrorism.

## est, estholes, and Spiritual Tyranny

In the previous chapter I alluded to est as a form of spiritual tyranny but did not name it. The idea of est is to bring about personal transformation. They make very loud noises about not being a spiritual group, but much of their material comes from Mahayana Buddhism and Hinduism. For a group that claims to be aggressively secular to the point of some trainers jumping up and down on a Bible or throwing one across the room in anger, est used a lot of spiritual material. (est has transformed itself into a kinder, gentler version called The Forum.)

During the 1970's and for a good bit of the 1980's at least one million people subjected themselves to est. This was both a highly refined yet an extremely blunt experience. Right from the beginning the trainees are called assholes, sticks, turkeys, and chicken shits. A complaint about the profanity is usually answered with "Go f\*\*\* yourself." The abuse is not strictly based on profane terms. Throughout the first and second days of the training, the trainees are called "hope fiends" and "ineffective humans". They were constantly reminded that nothing—absolutely nothing—was working in their lives.

I sat next to Ben, another journalist, and constantly commented to him that this was worse than anything I had ever experienced in a born-again Christian environment. Ben was Jewish and claimed that none of the lowest experiences in his Jewish upbringing could match what he was witnessing now.

If someone protested about anything, the trainer would walk down with his microphone and scream both into the face of the complainer and into the microphone:

"Who the f\*\*\* do you think you are?! Your f\*\*\*ing life isn't working. That's what you need to face instead of being some whining crybaby like you're being now. Stop the whining and be a man, for Christ's sake!"

Can you imagine what happened when someone in the group claimed that she didn't appreciate hearing the Lord's name taken in vain?

est is the closest thing I have experienced to what the early humans experienced under the spiritual terrorism of the pretender gods. These humans from thousands of years ago had no real choices. If they didn't want to fight in a "holy war," they were executed or tortured. If they complained about not having enough food, they were either executed or made to work harder. Go against the established belief system and you were tortured, assassinated, or let off easy with the fear of hell.

Complain at an est training during the first day, and the trainer and his well chosen allies will go against you and make you miserable. Complain on the third or fourth day and most of the *trainees* will turn on you.

Why? Because spiritual terrorism often works. It worked in our ancient past, and it still works today. The men who tortured alleged witches during the Salem witch trials terrorized their victims, but they genuinely believed that they were right in doing this because it would help drive out the so-called witch's demons. The only real demons during this period were the Puritan ministers who allowed such a holocaust to happen.

The same mentality was prevalent in est. They believed that their harassment, haranguing, and terror tactics were aiding the transformation of themselves and humanity. Yell and scream at them long enough, and their defenses would break down. Keep them from going to the bathroom and not letting them eat until the late evening was a brainwashing technique used by the North Koreans against their enemies during the Korean conflict of 1950-1953. If a person is thinking about controlling his bladder, the spoken ideas are more easily embraced.

While one would think that ministers, priests, and rabbis were the main perpetrators of spiritual terrorism, this just isn't the case. That award goes to some of the self-appointed gurus of the new age movement. Ministers, priests, and rabbis have to go to at least three years of graduate training before they can practice. During my seminary days, I not only learned a lot in the classroom, but also learned a lot preaching on Sundays, working with youth groups, and interacting with people who were having the same experiences. I got to make my mistakes and discuss them with my professors and fellow students. Despite the fact that I did not go into the pastoral ministry, I took those skills with me into my career as a college teacher.

Not so with the new age movement.

The new age movement is more like a happening. It is one of those cultural phenomena that appears to spring up from out of nowhere. While only a small minority of new age gurus are spiritual terrorists, the fact that they are unchecked and unregulated is a serious problem. Most of these new age gurus are self-appointed. No schooling or certification is needed to be one. All one needs to do is proclaim himself or herself a spiritual leader and then get people to follow.

The following example is representative of a very serious problem within the ranks of the new age movement. The majority of new age gurus sincerely want to help the people they are leading. However, some have learned that the more they tell people what they want to hear, the more successful they will become. Some of the "stars" of the new age movement charge $250 to $400 for a one day seminar. The person who channels an entity called Ramtha can earn up to $14,000 for a one-day seminar.

While these commercially oriented people concern me, what really frightens me is the spiritual terrorist. He or she uses the promise of enlightenment to spiritually terrorize the people who follow him or her.

Such is the case with Nahir, who had changed his name from James Bartlett. Nahir claims that he was visited by Mora, a woman from another planet in the Seven Sisters Pleiades star system. (One simply wouldn't believe how many people claim to be visited by alien beings from another planet. Most of them are harmless and even manage to tell good stories. This wasn't the case with Nahir.) Mora told Nahir that he had to prepare people for the horror that was coming to planet earth. She said, "The earth will be in shambles by 2012."

Nahir was a sexually active man, and gathered around himself a number of very attractive women. He promised them that they would be lifted off the earth by the Pleiadians, well in advance of the earth changes.

I saw this as a great story for my muckracking tastes. I visited the group a few times. Each time I went there, I saw the horror increasing. Nahir had an effective way of bringing people to his way of thinking:

"Your thinking isn't good, Ken. We need right thinking people with us. You know, there's only room for a small number of people when Mora's space ship lands. We're only going to take the best people. Right now, I don't think Mora would let you come with us. Your thinking right now is too Earth-based."

What Nahir never realized was that everyone's thinking was Earth-based. However, some very misguided people tend to believe that they are agents from other planets sent to bring more light to Earth. I have met at least a hundred of these people, and I don't see much light in them—unless inflated egos somehow produce light.

However, Nahir went even lower. He claimed that Mora had told him that Ken's wife should be his spiritual partner. This was a euphemism for, "I really like your wife and want to sleep with her."

This went one step further when Nahir began channeling Mora. What was interesting about Nahir and widely known at the time was that he needed to smoke copious amounts of marijuana before he could channel Mora. I saw the horror of this when Nahir wanted me to write a screenplay about his experiences with Mora. Here I was, planning to write an expose on one of the lowest forms of the new age movement, and the channeled Mora was telling me it was my duty. Otherwise, I would not be able to go on Mora's spaceship when the Earth was going through its period of horror. I was going through my own period of horror, and wasn't handling it very effectively. Nahir, completely stoned, had only a pathetic imitation of a female voice. I immediately asked myself how all these people could believe that Nahir was channeling the spirit of an extraterrestrial being.

When I said I could not write the screenplay, I received pressure from the group. Here I was, actually refusing the request of a "highly advanced" extraterrestrial. To top that off, Mora called me the anti-Christ, and claimed that I was doing great harm to the group. I never visited this group again.

*Chapter Five*

# The Slave Chip's Greatest "Victory" The Conversion Archetype

This chapter is speculative and is meant to stimulate thought rather than be stated as dogma. I thank the many psychologists I have as friends or have met at conferences who have helped me to develop this concept.

Something lies deep within us that creates a sense of profound transformation or spiritual conversion. At one point a person is in a normal state of consciousness; then they experience a profoundly moving event, after which everything is experienced in a different manner.

This is true of people who have had near death experiences. Many return to life profoundly changed. While some claim the experience was positive—entering a white light and speaking with spiritual beings—others claim that they experienced the horrors of hell and were relieved to be returned to their present life. With those who encounter a near death experience, most are profoundly changed. One example was a 16-year-old cheerleader who was so profoundly changed that she quit the cheerleading squad and found sports events to be boring.

## Was Something Placed into Our Brains?

What is interesting about these near death experiences is that they can be created by stimulating a certain area of the brain. The only thing missing is the white light. Could this mean that this experience is something that was put into our brains when we were created? If so, could the purpose of this have been a ploy of manipulation instead of a genuine spiritual experience? Could someone or some entity have created our brains in such a manner that this near death experience could kick in under certain conditions? Was there a much more manipulative agenda at work when this was placed in a certain area of our brain?

Remember that everything in the near death experience can be simulated by pushing on a certain area of the brain. What is significant is that *everything happens except seeing the white light*. Could the white light be the stimulus that initiates the near death experience? If this is so and this experience is genuine, why is it programmed into an area of our brains?

Something sounds fishy here.

The near death experience may be genuine, but it could also be part of the conversion archetype that simulates a conversion experience to set up people for manipulation.

People in organized religion should be noting is that the near death experience is not consistent. Christians see Jesus, Buddhists see Buddha, and Islamic people see Mohammed. People who have no religious background tend to see angelic beings. People from all of these backgrounds also have hellish experiences.

However, something much less known is another experiment mentioned in *Discover* magazine at the end of the 1980's. One doctor spent three years trying to prove that he could create powerful recollections of being abducted by aliens simply by stimulating the brain with electrodes and having a light flashing in a precise area right above the person's eye. Most claimed after the experience that they had profound and vivid memories of being abducted by aliens.

Does this mean that this is something else that is built into out brain structure?

If something is locked in our brain structure that can create near death experiences and the memory of being abducted by aliens, could we also have something built into our brain that stimulates the feeling of transformation? If so, this would be the conversion archetype.

John Wesley claimed to have a transformational experience when he felt his heart "was strangely warmed." From this experience he created what is now the Methodist Church. Martin Luther, a devout Catholic at the time, had a similar experience when reading the Bible. When he read the verse, "The just shall live by faith," he was instantly transformed and began a spiritual search that formed the early stages of the Protestant Reformation.

These occurrences feel wonderful. I encountered this when hearing an evangelist speak while going forth to accept Jesus as my personal savior with a group of others who were equally affected. Thirty years later I profoundly felt the presence of God within me while dancing. The experience so impacted me that I had to go outside and just be by myself. This was a different God that I experienced this time—a God of unconditional love instead of an angry God who would condemn you to hell if you didn't accept his TV dinner version of salvation.

Both were deeply moving experiences—the first being terrifying and cathartic, and the second producing a peace that passes all understanding.

Whether it was conditioned into out cellular memory thousands of years ago or actually instilled in our brain as something waiting to be stimulated, I simply don't know. I don't even know whether this is something good, bad, or neutral.

What I do know for sure is that spiritual tyrants wait in the wings to manipulate people right after they have had this experience. They may not know about the slave chip, but they do know that once a person has a conversion experience, they can be much more easily manipulated. Their intent, from their perspective, may be to deepen the experience. However, what most do is end up creating spiritual slaves.

Most people experience the conversion archetype during church services, revivals, and other evangelistic endeavors. The preacher or evangelist knows how to tap into this conversion archetype—even though he may not even know what it is. He will, however, claim that this was the force of God or the Holy Spirit moving people to experience this profound sense of need to covert.

One of the most pathetic things I experienced in my previous years as a fundamentalist Christian was seeing someone come forward to accept Jesus as their personal savior and then watch the vultures descend upon them within minutes, hours, or days:

> You've got to begin Bible study right now. Satan can take you right back.

> You must join a Bible believing church. Yours isn't good enough.

> You've got to give up dancing: it's a sin.

> Your boyfriend isn't saved. You must bring him to the Lord or leave him.

Poor God, he just isn't able to get things done. Thank goodness for all those people who step in and get it done for Him. If the Holy Spirit does indeed create the conversion experience, it is not the Holy Spirit who guides people when they decide to take over for God.

I try to stay away from people who have had a conversion experience. If they want to tell me about it, I find the narrative incredibly boring. I know that sounds very cynical, but I put these people in the same category of men of all ages who find great joy in talking about their sexual conquests. Listening to someone else talk about a sexual or a conversion experience are two areas where the narrator should pay the listener the going rate for psychologists.

However, the most difficult people to listen to are the conversion vultures who jump right on a recently "converted" person and begin pushing an agenda filled with rigid dogma. If any of those recently converted people want to talk to me, I know that their agenda is already fixed, and I am not interested. This is not insensitivity as much as the pain I endure watching people brainwashing themselves. They want be to be a part of it, and I just want to be somewhere else.

However, the same experience happens to people in humanistic psychology encounter groups. Confronted by the leader and others in the group, some experience a profound sense of release and a desire to change. Others claim that they feel free for the first time in their lives. This usually happens after an intense encounter group or a high energy weekend workshop.

John took one of these intensive weekend workshops called "Radical Love." John claimed it should have been called "Radical Shit." The leader of a group of 15 people gently and gradually began working up to a feverish pitch. What John didn't realize was that he was only one of eight people taking the workshop for the first time, leaving seven people waiting to work on John and the others.

John was uncomfortable enough with the leader screaming at the group and even more so when he began screaming at John:

"I'll bet you think you love people, don't you. I'll bet that you're convinced that you love your wife, but you don't!"

Then the leader turned to John's wife and let her have it.

"You're sitting there and crying because you feel so high and mighty. Lady, you don't love your husband, just like he doesn't love you!"

John was positive that he loved his wife, but the graduates in the group—those who had participated in the program previously and returned to help others through—had their "radical" version of love in mind for John. Nothing else qualified. They also had in mind that John have a conversion experience—just like they had during their time in the program. What John really could have used was to see those people who had completed the program, were not all that thrilled, and had demanded their money back.

Then the leader went right back to yelling at John:

> You claim that you love, but there's a price for that love. How many times have you said that you love Julie because she does something nice for you? How many times do you convey the unspoken message of "I will love you IF you do this for me"? You probably love Julie more after you have sex. Do you tell her you love her when she's throwing up after a wild party?

It got even worse when the participants were split into small groups. It was at this time that the graduates became truly confrontive:

> You really think that you love your children, don't you? I'll bet you have in your mind exactly what Julie and John Jr. should become. You probably want John to be just like you—an athlete. I'll bet you have him playing Little League right now. And why is he named John anyway? Couldn't you at least give him an original name! Good God, you want him to be another you. What kind of love is that?

Neither John nor Julie ran from all of this. Friends and graduates of the program had waxed lyrical about how life changing this experience would be. In the end, both thought the program had been a life-changing event. They had felt the conversion experience as a cathartic release that left both sobbing.

"I really want to love, but I feel so blocked," John sobbed.

Four of the group members hugged him, and he claimed he felt the best that he had felt in his life.

Weeks later both John and Julie claimed that their marriage was working better and that they had a profound understanding of love and intended to practice it for the rest of their lives.

However, a danger lurks with the conversion experience. It can divide as much as it joins. Julie was able to get back the feelings of her conversion experience by being part of the graduate groups and workshops for new people. When it came to confronting people, Julie was a natural.

"It's so wonderful to move those people into a more loving way of life," Julie said.

John, however, was becoming disenchanted. He went to only one of the new people workshops and quickly realized that he didn't enjoy bullying people into being more loving. Each additional graduate workshop was good only for getting together with people he liked. However, the material was boring and made him wish he were somewhere else.

Julie's zeal and John's increasing disenchantment began driving a wedge between them. Julie was now a true believer and insisted that John wasn't dedicated enough to Radical Love. The strife over this eventually caused them to separate and divorce. The irony was that they originally went to Radical Love to improve what both thought was a fairly good marriage.

## est—the Ultimate Conversion Archetype Experience

When Werner Erhard created est, he had this profound sense of transformation in mind. Of the over one million people who have taken est, more than 90% of them felt like they had experienced a profound change. Some talked to alienated parents for the first time in years—even decades. Others quit the jobs they hated. Some left their spouses immediately. Others claimed that they would give their spouses a chance at saving the marriage, but only if they took est as quickly as possible.

For those who think that the tactics of organized religions are oppressive, they pale in comparison to the est experience. People are not allowed to have watches, and all the windows are covered with dark paper so people don't know whether it is dark or light outside. During each day of the four-day experience, only one meal is allowed, and that usually occurs at 10:00 p.m. People are allowed to go to the bathroom only when the trainer tells them they can. During my est experience, the group had to wait for nine hours before having a bathroom break.

When one lady ran to the bathroom on her own, the trainer called her an "ungrateful cunt" for daring to go to without permission. People who took prescribed medicines were called "dependent babies" who were "enslaved by their doctor's whims." However, the people who were truly enslaved were those who voluntarily took est. (I took est as a journalist and therefore was allowed to eat when I wanted and go to the bathroom when I wanted. I didn't experience the transformation that is est's goal. People told me that I failed to "get it" because I was eating and going to the bathroom when I wanted).

Yet, more than 90% did experience some transformational moment. Many brought people to guest events where those who had already taken est went to the microphone and gave rousing testimonies as to how est had profoundly changed their lives.

Does any of this sound familiar?

The house is structurally the same, but it has a variety of colors.

# Chapter Six

# The Danger of Beliefs

## Belief and the God Box

So it is with much of the spiritual experience. People who insist that God fit into the well conditioned box that they have developed are setting themselves up for disappointment.

God is much bigger than the boxes that humans insist that "He" confine himself to. God doesn't want to confine "Himself" to a box anymore than "He" wants you to confine yourself to some spiritually correct belief box.

Humanity made a wrong turn thousands of years ago. In *Past Shock* I suggested that this turn was actually thrust upon us by technologically advanced beings. These beings realized that one of the best ways to manipulate humans and get them to work hard was for pretender gods to tell them what they needed to believe about these highly manipulative beings. Those who refused to believe that these technologically advanced beings were God found themselves punished severely—sometimes even put to death.

Watching a friend die is a "wonderful" way to condition people. The Inquisition is more recent proof of that. Both moments of history had one goal in mind: the instilling and protecting of belief systems. Unfortunately, this process tended to put the true God into a very narrow box.

The legacy of these alleged technologically advanced beings has stuck with us through history. The black moments of the Crusades and the Inquisition point out the insanity that humans will allow themselves to inflict in the name of spiritually correct belief systems. At the turn of the 18th Century, we burned witches in America because we believed that they were possessed by the devil. In that unfortunate time, pastors urged people to believe that a woman could come under the spell of the devil while working at her spinning wheel. Belief in this system was paramount, and it helped maintain an insane lifestyle.

Despite all this obsession and concern about belief, belief wasn't appropriate then, and it isn't appropriate now.

Belief stifles the spiritual experience.

Belief enhances spiritual slavery.

## Belief vs. Experience

When a person is searching for something to believe in, he or she is not really searching for a spiritual experience. Instead he is following a conditioned pattern which says, "I've got to find the correct cluster of beliefs if...

My life is going to work....

My soul is going to be saved....

I'm going to be worthy of God....

I am going to be worthy as a person"....

The person searching for that spiritually correct—and perhaps even spiritually liberating—cluster of beliefs rarely realizes that one only deepens one's spiritual slavery by pursuing beliefs rather than experiences.

The belief system is frozen like ice—perhaps having been frozen for thousands of years. It has no life to it other than the promise of eternal life in another experience beyond the grave. Beliefs are rigid. They claim that the mind must be in a certain frozen state in order to be worthy of a higher power. When the main priority is belief, essential experience gets negated and the rope of spiritual slavery tightens.

Beliefs are stultifying.

Like water that does not move, the end result of rigid beliefs is stagnation.

Only spiritual experiences can enrich a person's life.

I know people who are very sincere and have strong beliefs about God. They go to their chosen sacred books to learn exactly what they should believe. Poor God. If something in His/Her/Its nature dares to go against their well-established belief system, then that aspect of God simply will not—or actually cannot be—experienced. Sadly, some of these sacred books range from the obtuse to the impossible.

(The *Atra-hasis*, which I constantly quoted from and alluded to in *Past Shock*, is a difficult and repetitive book to read. The *Mahabarata* has lost out to the *Bagavad Gita*, most likely because the *Mahabarata* is the longest sacred book in existence. The Old and New Testaments don't come off much better. They, frankly, are very hard to read and cause one to wonder whether such demanding material could be the word of God.)

Because people are taught to believe that these sacred texts are indeed the true word of God, then anything outside of these sacred books is believed to be, well, ungodly. God could be seen as ungodly simply because His actions are believed not to be of the godly nature described in the ancient scared texts.

Poor God: he's stuck in an image fostered thousands of years ago. That truly is an illustration of Him being put into a belief box.

Thus, a belief in God can too often be an ecclesiastical insurance policy against the experience of God.

I saw belief taken to its extreme when my dear friends Fran and Greg stood on the edge of divorce. Fran claimed that God was leading her away from an abusive marriage, and had lots of Bible verses to support her view. Greg, on the other hand, felt that God was leading her to remain in the marriage—abusive as it was for Fran. He also had a plethora of Biblical citations urging an adherence to the wedding vows.

What Fran was experiencing was abuse—both physical and mental. She had been to marriage counseling with Greg, and still the abusive experiences continued. Based on her *experience*, Fran had very good evidence that no light existed at the end of the tunnel. Thus, based on years of abusive *experience*—and the promise of more to come—Fran decided to dissolve the marriage.

If Greg had been more into experience than belief, he might have been able to save his marriage. However, he had been conditioned from a young age to believe that the man was the ruler of the house, and the man's will should be followed—even when he is abusive. Greg's belief system made it okay for him to continue his abuse. Had he been focused more on experience than belief, he would have had the empathy for Fran to know what he was doing to her—and what she was feeling.

## Beliefs: An Insurance Policy Against Spiritual Experience

As heretical—and potentially blasphemous—as this sounds, beliefs are not the way to spiritual freedom. Instead, they guarantee spiritual slavery more than spiritual liberation.

If you want to experience spiritual liberation, you need to realize that your need to believe—and believe correctly—is standing in the way of your spiritual liberation.

Some will be shocked with such a pronouncement. Many will claim that I am deliberately trying to shock people in order to sell books. If I only wanted to sell books, I would stay within the spiritually correct belief system and convince them that the spiritual slavery they are experiencing is really spiritual freedom. That is one of the saddest aspects of the spiritual quest: gurus and spiritual leaders are pawning off spiritual slavery as spiritual freedom.

It's time for such insanity to end.

God created humans to be agents of free choice; he didn't give them agency and then expect them to choose a highly limiting "spiritually correct" cluster of beliefs. God is a creator, and he created humans to be free—and to be creative with that freedom. The fact that we have either conditioned ourselves to be spiritual slaves or have actually had that thrust upon us thousands of years ago, does not in any way change what God created us for: agents of free will who are meant to be co-creators with God.

The essence of spiritual slavery is keeping people locked up in highly limiting beliefs, like the following, that stultify the human experience:

We were born in sin.

We are fallen creatures and deserve to suffer because of the bad choices two people made thousands of years ago in the Garden of Eden.

We will burn in hell if we do not choose the "spiritually correct" cluster of beliefs that God has ordained.

We must suffer in this lifetime in order to have a better life in the next.

We must pay in this lifetime for acts that we committed in a previous lifetime.

*Chapter Seven*

# The Danger of Beliefs – Part Two

## How Beliefs Strangle Spiritual Liberation

Summing up some of the ideas presented here, this chapter moves more in the direction of pointing out some of the misguided beliefs that most humans have about God. So many people insist on seeing the entities described in their sacred books as God. This is tragic because many of these books were written at a time when the pretenders—a group of technologically advanced beings—were lying to the emerging human race. When they told these humans they were gods, they were lying. The warlord Jehovah went one step further and told his "chosen" people that he actually was the true God.

This is a sad concept because there is very little that is godly about Jehovah. He was a murderer who used frequent bouts of genocide to frighten his people into belief. He threw poisonous snakes into a group of starving people simply because they were complaining that they were hungry. He demanded that a man be stoned to death because he was picking up sticks on the Sabbath. He insisted that his well-trained armies rout the peace-loving Canaanites because he wanted that land for himself. He had a man and all of his family members brutally beaten to death simply because the man put two pieces of gold in his pocket while participating in the routing of Jericho. In the covenant that Jehovah made with the Israelites, he made it clear that if they did not go along with the agreement, that he would pay them back "sevenfold for their sins" and would cause them to be in such a state of starvation that they would *have to eat their sons and daughters in order to stay alive.*

The story of the Garden of Eden points out the fact that Jehovah was lying when he told Adam and Eve that they would die if

85

they ate of the forbidden fruit. The serpent claimed that they would see more clearly, and the serpent, rather than Jehovah, was the only one telling the truth. What Adam and Eve experienced in the Garden of Eden was a leap forward for humanity (despite the fact that Jehovah punished them brutally for daring to make this leap). They were the first to move from spiritual slavery to spiritual liberation. Rollo May in *The Courage to Create* has referred to the Garden of Eden as a fall upward. Ken Wilbur has expounded the same idea in *Up from Eden*.

Some reading this might be frightened by this concept and some of the things mentioned about Jehovah, which are all illustrated in the first five books of the *Old Testament*. However, the idea that humanity screwed up in the Garden of Eden is a belief that has hung on for too long and simply isn't true. What is true is that it was a very traumatic experience for Adam and Eve. This is the type of traumatic experience that eventually congeals itself into a frightening belief. It also creates a dangerous archetype and is deeply rooted in our collective unconscious. Moreover, this experience helped to create the spiritual slavery that permeates this planet. However, this stranglehold of "we're paying because Adam and Eve screwed up" is finally beginning to lose its hold on humanity.

One thing that Jehovah demanded of his followers was unquestioning belief. Yet, of all the people who believed in Jehovah as a God, Jehovah sure didn't believe in them. He used beliefs in a devastating way, creating warriors of bloody battles instead of creating warriors of the spirit. Jehovah demanded belief in him as God and threw in some additional, even more acute, requirements centering on total obedience to him. He demanded belief because he wanted to condition people to fight for him and do his dirty work. This work related mainly to fighting wars with enemies determined by Jehovah.

Even Christians are starting to realize that Jehovah was "kicking ass" rather than teaching a lesson. His punishment of Adam and Eve far exceeded the alleged crime. Bearing children in pain for the past twenty thousand years has no spiritual value whatsoever. Making

Adam and all his posterity "work by the sweat of your brow" has no spiritual value. All that appears to have come from these punishments is the overbearing Protestant/Puritan work ethic that, in many cases, has helped to turn some potentially fulfilling work into joyless toil. This is the act of a vainglorious warlord who dared to claim that he was God.

The true God simply would not punish people in this way.

Part of spiritual liberation is breaking free from the Jehovah concept of a mean spirited God who is really going to get us if we don't act exactly in the manner he prescribes.

## The Spiritually Correct Cluster of Beliefs

The idea of burning in hell for not having the spiritually correct cluster of beliefs is an idea that, sadly, refuses to go away. The fact that it is not even remotely linked to the truth has not stopped it. However, we can thank conditioning throughout history for this concept rather than God. The true God simply would not embrace such ungodly concepts.

God would not create creatures that he knew in advance were going to burn in hell.

God is not so petty that he would reject a person from happiness and a fulfilling life (in this or the next) simply because that person happened to be conditioned to believe a certain way.

God is not angry. That was Jehovah, the vainglorious pretender god. Therefore, the true God does not need to threaten people with eternal damnation in order to get them to shape up.

What keeps people locked in spiritual slavery more than any-thing else is the belief that once a person has *finally* come to his or her senses and accepts the "true" God, she now has a spiritual insurance policy. Once the person has the spiritually correct beliefs, spiritual experiences become less of a priority.

The feeling that one has finally "arrived" keeps people locked in spiritual slavery.

When I was "saved" at age thirteen, I got to feel superior to my hell-bound classmates, disgruntled neighbors, and particularly those "obnoxious Catholics" who wouldn't shut up about how spiritually superior they were. Knowing that all these Catholics en masse were going to hell gave me the most perverse spiritual delight. That was my thinking then. Now I get to watch college students five to fifteen years older imprisoned by the same belief system.

## How Beliefs Keep People in Hell

Because I was automatically going to heaven, I didn't have to think anymore. All I had to do was grow up, graduate from high school, go to college, get a job, get married, add a few children to the population, dote over my grandchildren—and then... and only then I could spend eternity resting in heaven.

What positively exhilarated me at age thirteen contributed to a deepening depression when I was thirty-three. I had just graduated from a fundamentalist seminary. Instead of being edified, my spiritual world was turned upside down.

I looked at expressions like the Greek word for "believe" (pis-teao eis) and realize that the word was more related to deep experience than belief, as we know it in the English language. The word "hell" (gehenne) was seen more as a garbage dump rather than some place deep in the earth or far out in space where people went to suffer for eternity. At this fundamentalist seminary I began to realize that the views that people had about hell being something experienced in an afterlife were actually keeping people in hell in this lifetime.

Put another way, the conditioned views that people had of hell as something experienced after one dies were keeping people locked up in spiritual slavery.

## Suffer Now—Rest Later

The idea that we must suffer in this lifetime so that we might be rewarded in a future lifetime is yet another idea that keeps people locked in spiritual slavery. Nothing in the Bible or most of the other sacred books suggests that this is an accurate view. In John 10:10, Jesus said, "I am come that you might have life and have it more abundantly." Whether this is a simple Rabbi or the Son of God, this is the essence of spiritual liberation.

The principle of having to suffer in the next life comes from Hindu ideology. Spiritual slaves dance to this view, claiming that a minor screw up will have to be paid for later. A major screw up means that you get to come back as a cockroach. (Sometimes when I am sitting in college faculty meetings bored out of my mind, I wish I were a cockroach.)

I know that some new age spiritual slave out there is reading that last sentence and thinking, "Be careful of what you wish for: you just might get it."

Spiritual slaves love to be sure that others not as "spiritually focused" as themselves are going to get their payback.

> You laughed at me when I had buckteeth, so you've got to come back in another lifetime with buckteeth. Now you will know what it feels like to be made fun of.

> You didn't give enough money to the church?
> That means you can't come back to a life in
> super-abundant America. Nope, you have to
> come as a peasant in rural Lithuania.

> You cheated the IRS out of money; now you
> get to come back as a tax collector.

Spiritual slaves entertain themselves with such diversions. Because they are not able to liberate themselves spiritually, they allow themselves to get smug about how others are going to pay for the evil they have done. This is the same mentality I had as a newly "saved" boy.

The spiritual slave remains in bondage because he or she needs to *believe* that those who have offended them are going to pay. What this belief overlooks is one of the most liberating concepts of spiritual freedom: the opportunity to forgive and forget.

## Beliefs—Untested but Still Accepted

For those who are feeling smug because they are locked into some new age or more liberal Christian tradition, consider the following stultifying beliefs.

> This planet is a school in which we are to learn
> lessons. If we don't learn the lessons the first
> time around, then we have to come back and
> learn them all over again—a kind of cosmic
> flunking out.

> We are here in this lifetime to work off karma
> accumulated from previous lifetimes. We have
> to keep coming out in other lifetimes until we
> have worked off all of our karma. However, in
> one of the greatest of cosmic absurdities, we

can actually build up more karma, when our intention was to work off past karma. What a deal!

We have been such bad boys and girls that aliens are here to save us from ourselves. These aliens are free to jab us with needles, stick implants deep up our sinus cavities, and plunge things deep up our anal orifices because they are the good guys, and we are the stupid ones.

Once one is spiritually free, he or she will no longer be subjected to the spiritually inferior concept that this planet is a school where we are to learn lessons. As long as that belief is maintained, one can justify continuing in life as a spiritual slave. The spiritually free person will exclaim, "This school really sucks; I'm outta here. I'm just going to enjoy myself."

As far as working off karma is concerned, that is a belief system that has long outlived its usefulness. If someone tortured you in a previous lifetime, I have two words for you: *forgive them.* If you were burned as a witch, burned at the stake, or made to rot in prison for the last ten years of your previous life, I have two other words for you: *forget it.*

Of course, if you want to keep living it again and again with a past life therapist, feel free to do so. You might find you are stimulating yourself, perhaps even providing stimulating conversation for others. However, if you continue it beyond what is needed for remembrance and healing, you are simply engaging in spiritual masturbation.

## Belief, Aliens, and Spiritual Slaves

I seriously considered whether or not to put something in this chapter about alleged alien abductions. An experience I had in

Berkeley, California made a tremendous impact on my life so I had no choice but to include it. I attended a one-day conference at the University of California Berkeley on alien abductions in October of 1992. There, five professors from various California state colleges— all of them Ph.D.'s—gave long speeches about how alien abductions were not only a reality, but that they are the best thing that can happen to us. They claimed that people were being abused for their own good, and that all resistance to any abduction should cease forthwith. Complete compliance was the order for these times.

About the only thing that these five didn't do was issue an altar call for us to come forward and accept these aliens as our personal saviors.

I couldn't believe the level of spiritual slavery that was coming from all five of these nationally known speakers. Dr. Richard Harder claimed that despite the negative quality of these experiences, it was essential that people surrender their free will and follow the agenda of the aliens. Dr. Leo Sprinkle claimed that humanity needs to be kicked around and have our butts kicked a few times by the aliens. This comes from the conditioned belief that we have to have our collective posteriors thumped mightily so that we might be saved from ourselves. One of them, Dr. Richard Boyland, has since lost his license to practice psychology, but this allegedly was not based on any views he had about alien visitors.

What a rallying cry for spiritual slavery!

Since that time I have written three articles for *New Perspectives Magazine* about the alien abduction phenomenon. In each of the articles I state honestly that I don't know whether aliens are here or not. If they are not here, we are making ourselves spiritual slaves to some phantoms we have created inside our heads. If indeed aliens are here, we are falling right into their hands by being such willing and compliant little spiritual slaves.

## Ignoring Evidence So Beliefs Won't Be Threatened

The sad fact is that anyone brave enough to read some of the writings recently discovered in archeological digs—as well as the material discovered in the past sixty years from the Dead Sea Scrolls and the Nag Hamadi Library—cannot help but come to the conclusion that humans, thousands of years ago, were conditioned to be spiritual slaves. To remain in a state of ignorance about these auspicious discoveries is to remain in a state of spiritual slavery.

A desire to read this material is a sign of spiritual exploration. A refusal to read this material because it doesn't fit into one's spiritually correct belief cluster is a sign of spiritual slavery. The justifiable claim that one is too busy to explore this material enables one to remain busy and continue an ancient counterproductive conditioning based more on belief than experience.

Too often, humans are pouring rancid wine into new wineskins.

We are spiritual slaves because we have been conditioned to be spiritual slaves. If, as all of Zecharia Sitchin's books have suggested, we indeed were created as a worker race, then we were created as slaves. Our spiritual liberation would have been the last thing on the minds of our "creators."

We were created thousands of years ago to work—not explore spiritual mysteries. In fact, the gods of the past did everything possible to keep humanity from exploring. Our spiritual liberation would have been seen as threatening to these pretender gods, who wanted us to do menial labor and eventually fight wars for these technologically advanced warlords. The fact that they lied to us by telling us that they were the true God only put us in a state of confusion—a state of confusion from which we still have not recovered.

## Beliefs and Hasty Closure

This confusion makes humanity as a species much more prone to belief than experience. Author William Harvey claims that the human mind is in such a state of spiritual confusion that it often overrides the needs of the person by injecting quick answers rather than correct answers. Harvey calls this condition "hasty closure." With hasty closure, the brain demands a quick resolution and actually sends out the false signal that a solution had been found.

This happened with Copernicus when he blazed trails—and nearly lost his life—for claiming that the Earth was not the center of the Universe. However, he stopped short of the truth when he claimed that it was actually the Sun that was the center of the Universe.

This happened with the brilliant Renaissance mathematician Johannes Kepler when, sitting with a group of his bored students, the brilliance of sacred geometry flashed into his mind with what he called "a brilliant light." Kepler's work advanced the science of mathematics, but Kepler made the mistake of considering it as gospel. Further research proved many of Kepler's concepts to be wrong.

This happens so often when people have genuine spiritual experiences. Instead of flowing with the experience and seeing where it leads them, they attempt instead to run the experience through already established belief clusters and end up sterilizing and eventually negating the experience. This is one of the greatest tragedies of the human experience.

The point of spiritual liberation is to break free of the conditioned spiritual slavery that has plagued us for thousands of years. Whether these technologically advanced beings that imposed this conditioning on humanity were extraterrestrials is irrelevant. Whether they came from another dimension or a parallel universe is beside the point. It doesn't really matter if this was an earth-bound race that eventually died out, returned to a home planet, or went forth to other stars.

What does matter is that how are we, as predominantly belief-bound spiritual slaves, going to move from this highly limiting condition into being experience-dominated and liberated spiritual beings?

That's what this book—in its own small way—is attempting to bring about.

*Chapter Eight*

# Malfunctioning Messiahs
# Past Shock's Unwanted Impact

One of the most significant examples of past shock fallout is the malfunctioning messiah. They appear as people of the cloth, new age leaders, leaders in the human potential movement, success gurus, far eastern religion gurus, and a host of others who want to control people rather than help them liberate themselves. While personal liberation is the title of their curriculum, personal enslavement is most likely their agenda. They only appear to offer true growth and few who follow them ever challenge them.

They are the sludge from Enlil, Jehovah, and a host of others from our ancient past who chose to enslave rather than liberate.

## What Is a Malfunctioning Messiah?

One of the chief traits of a malfunctioning messiah is that they are self-appointed. They quickly realize that there are hosts of people out there who are looking for answers. Our modern times have created increasing uncertainty, and this uncertainty causes people to look for answers—quick answers; even answers that can be crammed into a weekend workshop.

Another trait of the malfunctioning messiah is the *true believer*. The true believer is a person who needs to believe more than he needs to experience. Most true believers don't trust themselves to figure things out. They look for a belief system that can guide them through life.

This causes people to leave churches where the minister is simply preaching the gospel and go to churches that have the Christian experience already defined with 10 easy steps. Some evangelical Christians may go to a more intense fire and brimstone teacher who warns that the end is near and that his angrier version of God and Jesus must be followed. Some people will go from their chosen religion to a new age belief system carefully constructed by a malfunctioning messiah. Sadly, many of these malfunctioning messiahs get a lot of mileage from attacking organized religion. Their favorite targets are fundamentalist Christians.

What is (almost) unique about these true believer malfunctioning messiahs is that they insist that you believe what they believe. Only their fundamentalist rivals insist the same from their followers. They have found the truth, and you must adopt that truth. Failure to do so brings their disappointment or wrath.

Justin had heard that a massage therapist gave excellent massages. However, ten minutes into the massage, he realized that he was dealing with a malfunctioning messiah. As Diana was digging deep into his back, she suddenly went into a strange childlike voice. Frightened, Justin asked what she was doing.

In the same childlike voice, Diana said, "I am your inner child, and I want you to talk to me more. You hardly acknowledge me, and I feel so alone."

Justin was shocked. He didn't know what to say. He only knew that he wanted to get out of there. However, Diana and the "inner child" were adamant.

> Please talk to me. I feel so alone and want
> you to nourish me. You are so serious, and I
> don't have any fun. I feel trapped inside you,
> and you won't do anything for me.

Diana went back to her regular voice and informed Justin that he was really blocked and that by blocking his inner child he was endangering it. Jason was lying naked under a sheet, and all he wanted to do was get up and run. However, Diana didn't let up:

> You can't believe what is going on with your body. You are really blocked. All this energy is blocked in your muscles, and it is screaming to come out. Your inner child can guide you in this.

Diana, back in her own voice, told Justin that he had to set his inner child free and gave specific instructions on what his inner child was telling him to do. This included eating hot fudge sundaes, swimming nude in the ocean, dancing around the house, and crying more.

Another trait of the malfunctioning messiahs is that they genuinely believe that they are on a mission from God. This is not the true God, although they believe that it is. This is usually a god that they had been conditioned to believe in or a new-found god discovered in a new church or at a new age function. Some people in the new age movement feel it is fashionable to believe that *they* are God. However, most of these people believe that everyone else is too... 6,000,000,000 gods—now there's a happy thought.

However, this mission from god actually dominates these self-appointed messiahs and causes them to malfunction. Their problem is that they don't ask for God's guidance. Instead, they assume that they already know what God wants. Their view of God is a very narrow one. He's really pissed, wants redemption and warns that time is running out. This "time is running out" gambit has been used for at least 2,000 years. After the death of Jesus, people genuinely believed they were in the final days, and a host of malfunctioning messiahs jumped into the fray and frightened people into thinking that time was running out.

What most people fail to realize is that 15 other crucified and resurrected saviors before Jesus said almost exactly the same things he did and share the same general story. Some go back more than 6,000 years. Claiming that we are in the final days is an effective manipulation tool for those who would rather control than lead. With some of the malfunctioning messiahs, you are damned if you do and damned if you don't. People who break free of new age or religious tyranny feel they have moved on to something better. However, a lingering guilt lies right underneath their consciousness:

> If I don't return to my faith, I will burn in hell.

> I've experienced a lot of growth, but I might be on the wrong path.

> This meditation might be leading me away from God.

## The Harm That Malfunctioning Messiahs Do

The greatest harm that malfunctioning messiahs do is present a very twisted view of God. I have heard some new age leaders claim that God provided the sex drive so that his people could have fun. One Native American spiritual leader claimed that the heightened sex drive we have was a gift from the Sumerian god Enki, who realized that the worker/slaves were working hard and that sex was the reward for working so hard.

On the other side of the coin are those who claim that sex is evil unless it is used for procreation. Here we have the absurdity of a twenty-five-year-old single person who is supposed to hold back until he finds the right person to marry. This is bad press for the true God. He would never create humans who began being sexually aroused at age 11-13 and then were expected to be chaste until marriage. This is insanity that began when the pretender gods created us. They wanted to be absolutely sure that we procreated to generate more workers and made damn sure that the sexual drive was intense. This is one of the greatest examples of past shock.

One of the most "effective" ploys of malfunctioning messiahs is their ability to cause people to feel guilt about things that don't demand remorse. Most feel that this relates only to organized religion, but manufactured guilt goes far beyond the boundaries of religion.

When I attended Werner Erhard's "est" as an observing journalist, I could not believe what I was seeing. Under the rule of "est", people were harangued for failing to keep absurd commitments, running to the bathroom, and complaining that they were hungry. Bathroom privileges occurred infrequently, sometimes going nine hours between breaks. The only time that people got to eat during the day was at 10:00 p.m. I observed Roger, the trainer, as Jehovah returned. Past shock was in full force during the full four days of "est"; however, I doubt if Jehovah used as much profanity or humiliated people as much as Roger. Believe it or not, Jehovah actually had times of compassion for his people, as few and far between as they were.

Once one completed "est" and went home, harassment was intense for taking the next graduate workshop. Even though I was a journalist and observing, I was harassed incessantly with demands, not requests, that I take the next workshop. To these twenty different people who would not let up with such demands, I was still incomplete and needed further work.

## The Creation of a Spiritual Holocaust

The proliferation of cults in the last 30 to 40 years is frightening. Most cult leaders know how to tap into the ancient past shock conditioning. Having these skills, most cult leaders can make very good money utilizing this conditioning for their own gain.

Cults prey on genuine seekers and true believers. The cult leaders are very adept at spotting incomplete people and bringing them into the fold. What the cult leaders are not very proficient at is sensing *their own* incompleteness. Most cult leaders are malfunctioning messiahs who have found a way of getting rich and filling their own lack of completeness by making others more incomplete.

Not only do some cults demand turning over their savings accounts and the deeds to their homes, but some also forbid any further contact with members' parents or families. Joe Riley, one of my best friends, flew from California to Florida in an attempt to see his only daughter Sally, a member of one such cult. Ken, her cult leader, met Joe at the gate and said that seeing Sally would not do him any good. Joe was at the point of tears as Ken explained that he had become her new father. Joe went home without any communication with his daughter.

If I wanted to start a cult, I could become a millionaire within two years. Some have done it in less than a year. However, I would have to stop shaving because I would not be able to look at myself in the mirror.

One of the greatest ironies of cult leaders is that they genuinely believe they are liberating people. Demanding that they never have contact with their families is seen as liberating them from people who are possessed by Satan. Starving them with a protein deficient diet frees them from being influenced by anything other than the narrow "God" of the cult leader. Depriving them of sleep does the same. Screaming dogma at them for long hours frees them from past conditioning and substitutes a much more devastating one.

Cults are indeed a spiritual holocaust.

In the 1970's David Moses founded the Children of God cult. In 1972 I visited with some of their leaders and found them to be okay as people, but their dogma frightened me. Later in the 70's and into the 80's, David came up with one of the most heinous concepts ever developed by a cult leader. He created "flirty-fishing": using young, attractive—often underage—girls to lure people into the cult with the promise of sex. In the beginning David thought that sex was something to be avoided. Now he was using it to lure people into the Children of God.

I had the impact of this come crashing down upon me when a member of the cult named Paul Saran came to lecture to two of my critical thinking classes. He described how his youngest daughter was put out on the streets to offer sex to men who would come to Children of God meetings. Paul described how doing this made his daughter a psychological mess, attempting suicide many times. He broke down crying and took several minutes to regain his composure. He bravely admitted that he had urged her to do this at the command of David Moses. At the time he felt he was doing God's will.

Between the two classes, his daughter had made yet another attempt to take her life.

If this isn't a spiritual holocaust, I don't know what is.

## How to Spot a Malfunctioning Messiah

Malfunctioning messiahs are difficult to spot for the average person. Most are charming, beguiling, and charismatic. They have a gift of drawing people to them. Because they save the dogmatic and controlling material until one is well entrenched in a cult, everything is new and exciting. The leaders appear as positive and charismatic people. One doesn't hear anything bad about them until the damage is done. Even then, few people challenge them. The law can't touch most of them because religious freedom is guaranteed in the Constitution.

However, there are some traits that you can look for, and if you see a group of these traits, you are looking at a malfunctioning messiah.

**First**, they cannot see you as happy. No matter how much you might protest, you need what the "messiah" is offering. What is strange is that if you attend the weekend workshop, join a weekly class, or become part of a group where other opinions are not tolerated, members or the malfuctioning messiah will insist that you look worse than they do. They will attempt to make you feel as badly as they think you look—until you reach the point where you actually believe them.

**Second,** no matter how well your life is going, the "messiah" still sees you as needing to be fixed. According to them, if you adopt their dogma, chant their chants, or attend their weekly Bible study then things will get better. If you stop coming, bad things that happen in your life are blamed solely on that decision. One leader of a Bible study claimed that the Holy Spirit was guiding her to tell one person that if she didn't come more frequently, she would have a horrible accident.

Poor Holy Spirit.

**Third,** If you go to a meeting of a " malfunctioning messiah," the people in the meeting are perky rather than happy. There is an energy that seems forced rather than genuine. Some new age groups demand that their members stand and applaud for their leaders for five minutes at a time. This is heavy duty conditioning—just like in the ancient of days.

**Fourth,** within a "messiah" group, you find you gain acceptance only when you say what conforms to their dogma. Admittedly, this is true is most areas of the human experience. However, the acceptance is really turned up in these groups, and it can be quite beguiling.

**Fifth,** be very wary of any "messiah" who tells you that God likes certain things and disapproves of other things. This was true of the old gods—Zeus, Enlil, Yahweh/Jehovah—but it is not accurate in regards to the true God. Instead, this eventually becomes a tool of manipulation and control—especially if the "messiah" claims to speak for God.

**Sixth,** anyone who asks you for money is to be avoided. You are their means of becoming very rich. This does not apply to churches where people willingly pledge money to support the church—after such offerings the minister does not get to keep the money. Malfunctioning messiahs do.

**Seventh**, beware of anyone who claims that they are speaking directly for God. The true God speaks through the soul of individual people. I cover this more thoroughly in my upcoming book, *Freedom From Religion*.

**Eighth**, be very wary of people who ask you loaded questions:

Do you love the Lord?

Haven't you had enough of your oppressive religion?

Have you been washed in the blood of the Lamb?

Aren't you tired of your dogmatic beliefs?

When are you going to let go of all that is blocking you from being free?

What planet are you from?

I have been asked that last question many times. The first time I encountered it was when I attended a Unarius conference on UFOs in San Diego in 1980. My passion for learning about UFOs was high then. Entering the auditorium, I was asked, "What planet are you from?" I answered "earth" and this person looked at me strangely. Finally he said, "You have to sit in the back row."

At this conference, people were allegedly from 33 different planets and were dressed in appropriate costumes related to the person's planet. The more spiritually advanced the planet was, the closer you got to sit to the front. This is yet another form of manipulation by "messiahs" who claim to be getting their information from space beings.

**Finally**, be very wary of "messiahs" who channel material from space beings or earth-bound spiritual beings. Another category is "light beings." They are unique because they have never had an experience in matter. How can someone who has never incarnated on Earth be taken seriously? They know nothing about the earth experience. It's like watching *ER* and then thinking that qualifies you to advise doctors about how to do surgery. My command to these light beings is, "come down for a few lifetimes on earth and experience pain, junior high school, and genital itching, and then I might—just might—be willing to hear what you have to say."

Some channeled material can be edifying. An excellent example of this is *A Course in Miracles,* which contains thought provoking material. But I am suspicious about its origins and much of its advice. I have seen some leaders of this material claim that it has the same truth as the Bible. Others claim it was written by Jesus—which I find suspicious. If this is presented as dogma rather than material worth thinking about, then the leader is a malfunctioning messiah.

Trust nothing that comes from the alleged Space Brothers. Most of it is rambling and often insulting to the average person's intelligence. The fact that two to three million people might be reading and listening to this channeled material is truly frightening.

Is a minister, priest, or rabbi a malfunctioning messiah because he insists that the Bible—Jewish or Christian—is the word of God? No. Most men and women of the cloth believe this themselves and state their belief. Most are aware of the fact that some in their congregation don't believe this and are fine with it. I firmly believe that such holy books are the words of men rather than being directly from God. At the same time, most priests are not intentionally manipulative or controlling when they claim that the Bible is the word of God. It is a manipulation that has been carried down for so long that it is now a sincere and accepted belief.

As a parting note, the meaning of the word "messiah" has been generally thought to mean, "anointed one". However, 5,000 years ago it had a much stronger meaning: "the dragon."

## Chapter Nine

# A Short Course in Dealing with Zealots, Fanatics and Spiritual Tyrants

Zealots, spiritual tyrants, and fanatics (religious and otherwise) are not going to go away. In fact, their ranks are increasing at an exponential rate. However, certain techniques do work to avoid succumbing to their efforts.

First of all, I do not believe that most Mormon missionaries and Jehovah's Witnesses are fanatics. I admire their courage to go door to door and experience what often is hostile rejection. I made a commitment long ago that I would not be one of the people who would make life unpleasant for them.

However, a few from each group have been pushy and I have developed some survival skills for dealing with them. What has worked well for me is asking them:

Do I have an equal chance of convincing you that you are wrong as you have of convincing me that you are right?

This stops most of them because they have never really thought about this. They come with the truth, and now someone is going to attempt to convince them that they don't have the truth. Being a college professor gives me an edge in this area.

I mention to Jehovah's Witnesses that their prophecy of the world ending in 1914 didn't happen. Most are not aware of that fact.

If Mormon missionaries get aggressive with me, I'm not going to talk to them until the rest of the Golden Scrolls are translated. Only one-third of them were translated; the other two-thirds remain untranslated or unreleased to the public. However, few of the Jehovah's Witnesses and Mormon missionaries are aggressive. Most respect a person's right to say no and move on. It is the newly converted that are the hardest to accept your request to move on. With the ultra-aggressive, I simply say that I don't want to go to heaven. Shakespeare, Steinbeck, and Boccacio won't be there. Heaven strikes me as boring, I claim. It's going to be much more fun in hell. In fairness I do tell these well-meaning people that I do not believe in the Christian concept of heaven and hell.

However, these ploys—while effective—are also devious. The best way to deal with fanatics, zealots, and spiritual tyrants is to insist that they use critical thinking skills when presenting their case. This is particularly effective when one is trapped in a group of people or at a dinner gathering where someone is dominating the conversation with "the true beliefs."

## What Exactly is Critical Thinking?

Getting an exact definition of what critical thinking is is such a difficult task that not even the authors of twenty different textbooks about critical thinking could agree. Don't let that discourage you or cause you to lose your zest for understanding critical thinking. It is a wonderful antidote for thinking that is dominated more by blind belief or conditioning rather than by experience.

I was a college teacher who taught critical thinking. Most college professors who teach critical thinking agree that one of the most important aspects of critical thinking skills is the ability to suspend judgment until one gets the facts.

One of the most unique experiences I had in one of my critical thinking classes was during the first day of class. Two students were arguing about me. One was convinced that I was trying to convert her into becoming a Christian; the other was positive that I was trying to destroy his Christian faith. Old, non-thinking habits die hard. Suspending judgment for a few more classes was called for here.

In one of my critical thinking classes, I had a student walk out after 15 minutes of the first day of class. However, she did not go gently into the night. At the door she fumed that I was an instrument of the devil for saying what I was saying. The best she could muster up for a balanced view was claiming that I also was an instrument of God because I had "inspired" her to go more deeply into her Christian faith and read the Bible more.

Another student, Larry, came into my office full of religious conversion zeal and asked if he could talk to me about how bringing Jesus into my life would make my life much better. I responded with what I considered to be balance:

> I'd be willing to listen to you talk about that for ten minutes if I can talk to you about why I think Jehovah was psychotic.

Larry danced around my office screaming, "Time out, time out" complete with referee gestures. He thought the idea was preposterous. I explained to him that I didn't think the idea that Jesus could make a difference in my life was preposterous—that I was willing to suspend judgment until I heard what he had to say. I simply asked him to give me the same courtesy—which he refused to do.

The greatest crisis to come from the unwillingness to suspend judgment is what Americans did in the 1980's when we rushed to judgment thinking that AIDS was a disease predominantly limited to homosexuals and I.V. drug users. This was believed by most of the medical community, despite the more accurate truth, found later, that it was a contagious virus affecting more people than first thought. That initial, limited belief, some doctors tell me, prompted the death of at least 200,000 people who could have otherwise been saved.

I have found this example to be quite effective when dealing with people who refuse to suspend judgment. This could be a newly converted acquaintance or a parent who thinks that I am leading their son or daughter astray. When someone says that AIDS is a punishment from God, I withdraw from the conversation knowing that it is futile. I have brought up that God appears to be sexist because "He" is killing more men than women.

Rushing to judgement often feels good. Jumping to conclusions is what many do when talking about organized religion. Religions are often stereotyped based on the actions of more zealous members. For example, very few right to life people felt good about a doctor who performed abortions being killed by one of the more rabid of their ranks.

## Recognizing Faulty Thinking

Recognizing someone's faulty thinking and then making him or her aware of it has about the same impact as correcting a person's grammar in public. I have taught English Composition, Literature, and Critical Thinking, but I never corrected a student's grammar or claimed they spoke a fallacy in class. However, knowing where faulty thinking exists can be very helpful—especially if you are at a crossroads in your life.

## Faulty Thinking Example Number One—Wishful Thinking

Wishful thinking shows up in history. An excellent example is when the British Prime Minister made a pact with Hitler, and then went home claiming that England would never be attacked by Germany. He should have known better. When it comes to past shock and its devastating impact, one needs to look closely at the fallacy of wishful thinking.

The promise of heaven is an example of wishful thinking. It may exist, but it cannot yet be proven. It survives as a concept because people want to believe that they are going to go to a wonderful place after they die.

The hope that life will be better after a conversion experience is an excellent example of wishful thinking. The far eastern religions do a much better job of preparing people for the crash that comes after a conversion experience. The fact is that little can match what the conversion experience has provided. Life goes on, and that peak experience cannot be brought back at will. Knowing this ahead of time can prevent a lot of pain.

Telling a recent convert that you want to see if they have the same zeal a year later is not an unreasonable request. I tell Christian zealots that the recently converted Paul of Tarsus was ordered by Aninais to wait for three years before going out and preaching.

## Faulty Thinking Examples Numbers Two and Three—Ad Hominem and Guilt by Association

Ad hominem is probably the most "popular" of the faulty thinking areas. It causes a person during an argument or discussion to make an irrelevant personal attack on the person promoting the idea rather than discussing the issues at hand.

New age leaders have had a field day with this one. If you are reading a book that a spiritual leader disapproves of, some spiritual leaders will attack the author rather than the book's issues. I actually had one "spiritual leader" tell me that another "spiritual leader" was not to be trusted because in a previous lifetime in Egypt he (the other) had been a priest of Amun rather than the true god, Aton.

Some Christians attack *A Course in Miracles* because it is channeled material by, God forbid, a Jewish woman who was non-religious or, as some claim, an atheist. A minister's admonition not to trust anything another person says tells more about the minister than the other person.

When experiencing these ad hominem attacks by a fanatic, zealot, or spiritual tyrant, you can simply say, "Can we discuss the issues rather than the person?"

## Faulty Thinking Example Number Four—Appeal to Ignorance

Appeal to ignorance is easy to spot in other people but difficult to spot in oneself. For example, two people could be arguing about which religion is true:

DARLENE: I've never seen a personal appearance of this Allah that you claim is the true God. Therefore, I doubt very much that Allah exists.

DEVI: Well, I've never seen a personal appearance of your God, and that proves that He doesn't exist either.

Both people are using appeal to ignorance to "support" their claims. The fact that someone is ignorant of something is used as proof that what he is ignorant of does not exist or has no reality for him.

Just as it is hard to prove that God exists, it is equally hard to prove that God does not exist. One with good critical thinking skills realizes that it is difficult to prove something without hard evidence. Claiming that proof exists because it is written in the Bible is a fallacious appeal to authority.

## Faulty Thinking Example Number Five—Fallacious Appeal to Authority.

A correct appeal to authority is when you go to a doctor, discuss your symptoms, and then get a diagnosis. He might be wrong at times, but he is a genuine authority. A fallacious appeal to authority is going to a psychic, asking what to do about your medical problem and having the psychic channel a discarnate entity to tell you what to do. Just because the alleged spirit is in the etheric realms does not mean it can help you.

One of the areas where I have brought up fallacious appeal to authority is when someone quotes the Bible to me, assuming that we both accept it as the word of God.

Below is an example of an interaction I have had many times with people in my college office, on radio shows, or at lectures on my book:

> Allen: Your ideas are straying from what's presented in the Bible. The Bible says that Man is a fallen creature.
>
> Jack: Allen, you are doing the radio audience and myself a great disservice by assuming that everyone thinks the Bible is the word of God.
>
> Allen: Well, it is.
>
> Jack: To me, it's not. At one time I believed as you do, but years of research have led me to give up that belief.
>
> Allen: The Bible says that we are fallen creatures because Eve caused Adam to eat of the Tree of Knowledge.
>
> Jack: Allen, you are asking me to accept something that I don't think comes from a genuine authority. How would you feel if I asked you to accept the Sumerian *Atra-hasis* as the word of God?
>
> Allen: That's ridiculous. Only the Bible is the word of God.
>
> Jack: Then why did Moses take so much from the *Atra-hasis* when he was allegedly writing the book of Genesis?

I suggested that the only way the conversation could legitimately continue was for me to consider that the Bible might be the word of God and for him to consider that it might not. Otherwise, the conversation would be polluted with fallacious appeals to authority. I also urged him to realize that when he said, "The Bible says...", it meant one thing to him and something totally different to other people in the radio audience.

When dealing with people who claim to have the true authority, you can insist that you do not consider that particular sacred book, idea of God, or channeled entity to be a legitimate authority and suggest the conversation move to another area. If people continue to use a fallacious appeal to authority, simply remove yourself from the conversation.

## Faulty Thinking Example Number Six —Stereotyping

Stereotyping is when one sees the behavior of a few people from a certain group, culture, or religion and assumes that all members of the group act that way. Mexicans are lazy. Jews love money. All Irish people drink a lot. Scandinavians are sexually loose. It goes on and on, but it can be highly manipulative when zealots, fanatics, and spiritual tyrants resort to stereotyping.

New age people are the target of many fundamentalist Christians because of the excesses of a few.

Fundamentalist Christians are the target of new age people for the same reason.

Both sides aren't using critical thinking skills because they are judging the whole group by the actions of a slim minority. Mentioning this flaw to someone lost in habitual stereotyping is a good way to make spiritual tyrants more honest.

Within the ranks of the new age movement, some real excesses of stereotyping exist. Within the ranks of organized religion, some real excesses of stereotyping exist. Once you recognize them, you can call people on what they are doing.

# APPENDIX A

## The Foundation of *Past Shock*

Close to 12,000 years ago a race of technically advanced beings was on this planet. According to best-selling researcher/author Zecheria Sitchin, these beings came here 400,000 years ago. Both mythology and holy books support this: more than 30,000 written documents tell of a group of advanced beings who either came to Earth or already were living on Earth. These documents—especially the Sumerian, Assyrian, and Babylonian writings—claim that these beings came to mine precious metals. Whether they came from outside the Earth or from another part of this planet is not really an important issue at this point. As the supply of precious metals began to deplete, the work became more demanding, and the miners became mutinous. The *Atra-hasis* is amazingly clear in this area:

> Let us confront our chief officer
> That he may relieve our heavy work...
> Excessive toil has killed us,
> Our work is heavy, the distress much.

In this amazingly complex work, the *Atra-hasis*—and many other "mythological" works—tells of long negotiations to prevent a bloody mutiny. Finally, the advanced beings decide on a solution to their problems:

> Let a Lulu (primitive worker) be created...
> While the Birth Goddess is present,
> Let her create a primitive worker.
> Let him bear the yoke...
> Let him carry the toil of the gods!
> *Atra-hasis*

Who was that primitive worker species? None other than what is today referred to as *Homo sapiens*. Yes, we are the species that was created to "do the toil of the gods."

114

What happened is the Annunaki (as the gods were called in the Babylonian, Assyrian, and Sumerian epics) crossed its genes with the genes of an animal that resembled them. That animal creature they used is what we now refer to as *Homo Neanderthalis* (Neanderthal Man). What the Annunaki created from Neanderthal was Cro-Magnon Man. For millions of years Neanderthal man had no written language or capacity for an elaborate vocabulary. Cro-Magnon man had this capacity almost immediately. Cro-Magnon Man was a genetic cross between the old level of man and the gods. If we had only been "good little workers" and stifled our god-like nature, we would not have brought down the wrath of the gods. However, something happened in this experiment that the gods were not counting on.

## The Disastrous First Experiment

The genetic creation of humanity was not initially successful. Results were similar to the disastrous "killer bee" experiment performed in South America more than thirty years ago. The original intention of the scientists was to cross the genes of a stronger bee with the genes of a bee that was more prone to work harder. Instead, they created a very rebellious bee with killer instincts and a strong tendency to migrate. What the Annunaki wanted was a docile primitive worker who was smart enough to do menial work but not smart enough to discover that it was being exploited. Like the killer bee, *Homo sapiens* turned out to be very bright, innovative, and quite hostile to the idea of doing menial work. This initial group was bright—probably much brighter than we are now.

As a species we were so bright that we severely frightened our creators. They wanted us to do menial work in the mines, and we wanted to discover the secrets of the universe. If our creators had possessed a shred of spiritual evolvement, they would have nurtured us from our inception. However, their only intent was to exploit us. Thus, conflict erupted.

We rebelled against the idea of doing their dirty work. Eventually, they wanted us to fight wars for them, and we rebelled against that. This is clearly recorded in the *Old Testament,* other holy books, and in other ancient writings. This consistent theme runs through all of the past writings from all parts of the world. We were smart. Many of us may have been smarter than our own creators—and that must have severely frightened them. Then we started doing things that only increased their fears.

In *The Twelfth Planet* Zecheria Sitchin tells of a group of early humans in Babylonia that was so intelligent that it built a rocket ship capable of escaping the Earth's orbit. (Remember that the *Atra-hasis* and other ancient epics state that these gods claimed to come from the stars.) The gods were terrified that their newly created species might get back to the gods' homeland and tell of this infraction of the prime directive —not to interfere with any indigenous species. Thus, the gods got together and worked out a plan to prevent this:

> Come, let us go down and confound their language,
> that they might not understand one another's speech.
> (Genesis 11:7)

According to Sitchin, the above account is a more accurate version of the Tower of Babel story. Early humans were not building a tower as much as they were building a launching pad. Our getting free was something they could not allow, and they came down upon us brutally. Thus began the foundation of past shock.

## ANOTHER VIEW OF THE GARDEN OF EDEN MYTH

### What Really Happened at the Garden of Eden

Freud, Jung, and other founding fathers of psychology claim that even if the events of the Garden of Eden myth *didn't* happen, its impact as myth is still a gaping wound in our collective consciousness. Author Richard Heinberg in *Memories and Recollections of Paradise* relates how the human experience is shaped by our guilt for having been thrown out of the Garden of Eden. The consensus reality is that

God threw them out because they dared to eat of the Tree of Knowledge. It goes on to state that this was the beginning of sin and the point where the fall of man began. The problem with this consensus reality is that it is wrong. Instead, it was the beginning of a spiritual rape from which we are still shuddering (or at least blocking out).

Something did happen in the Garden of Eden — something very horrible. One of the gods, a pernicious pretender to divinity who called himself Yahweh (Jehovah), got totally caught up in his perverse paternalism and decided that Adam and Eve would be better off as cosmic, domesticated pets. The needs of these two people would be provided for as long as they remained at this level.

Adam and Eve were intelligent beings who were told to keep their lights under a bushel. Then, into the picture came a creature who thought Adam and Eve were getting a bad deal. Throughout history this creature has been greatly maligned. Some even claim that it was Lucifer, but not even the *Old Testament* calls him by that name. Instead, he is referred to as the Serpent. In most mythology and holy writings from throughout the world the Serpent is known as the purveyor of wisdom. For example, the Chinese saw both serpents and dragons as godlike, beneficial creatures who advanced humanity.

However, the Serpent has received very bad press from the Judeo-Christian segment of humanity. They saw — and continue to see — the serpent as evil, even as the devil. What the holy books do agree upon is that the serpent was very beautiful. Actually, it is amazing how much of the original story is left in the *Old Testament*.

Adam and Eve are told by Jehovah that they can have everything they want as long as they don't eat any fruit from the Tree of Knowledge. For them, this was equivalent to being told that you can have everything you want as long as you don't expect more than minimum wage and don't complain about the working conditions. They were told that if they ate of the fruit of the Tree of Knowledge, they would die.

This was a lie.

The Serpent appears and tells them that if they eat of the Tree of Knowledge their knowledge will increase significantly. At this point, the serpent is like Prometheus— about to steal fire from the gods and give it to humanity. Unlike Jehovah, the Serpent is telling the truth. His aim is not to destroy Adam and Eve as much as it is to liberate them.

What followed contributed greatly to past shock. Jehovah comes into the garden and says, "Where are you, Adam?" (something awfully strange to be stated by an omniscient God). Once Adam comes out of hiding, he observes a most traumatic event. Before Adam and Eve's eyes the Serpent is violently assaulted and mutilated—not something one would expect from an all-loving God, but unfortunately quite typical for the psychotic Jehovah. Other holy books describe an even more horrific fate for the Serpent: books like the *Jewish Pseudepigrapha* and *The Secret Book of John the Gnostic* tell of the Serpent brutally having each of its limbs hacked off and having to crawl on its belly from that time forth.

Then, of course, came all the other "prizes": women suffering in childbirth, men having to work by the sweat of their brow, and other multiplications of sorrow and pain. This was not the act of a loving god; this was the heinous act of a mentally tortured warlord who dared to tell his new "creations" that he was God. This expulsion from paradise was traumatic; however, it was also the beginning of humanity's liberation. (Ken Wilber's excellent book *Up From Eden* effectively discusses this thesis. Rollo May also touches upon this thesis in *The Courage to Create*.)

## BACK TO THE DRAWING BOARDS

### The Spiritual Rape Intensifies

One theme stands out in the thousands of mythological and holy writings: our creators did not like the way they originally created us. We were too smart and—from their perspective—too arrogant. We refused to become domesticated and we complained incessantly. The *Atra-hasis* tells of one of the gods who had enough:

The god Enlil said to the other gods:

> Oppressive have become the pronouncements
> of Mankind. Their conjugations deprive me of
> sleep.
>
> *Atra-hasis*

Being old enough to have suffered through three years of Latin studies, this writer finds perverse humor in this. However, Enlil (whom many claimed was Jehovah) sees no humor in the wailing pronouncements of his newly created worker race. Something had to be done. A new creation was needed: a dumbed-down worker human. They had already created spiritual rape by advancing us too quickly; now they were going to "de-advance" us.

The gods were mentally imbalanced Rodney Dangerfields who felt they just didn't get enough respect. Not only did they want workers who didn't complain, they also wanted us to venerate and revere them. While this is also a dominant theme in ancient writings, the one that best describes this "dumbing down" is the Mayan *Popul Vuh*. This holy book not only tells how the gods created humans as a work force, but also how they had to keep recreating humanity:

> We have already tried with our first creations,
> our first creations, our first creatures, but
> we could not make them praise and venerate us.

> So let us try to create obedient, respectful
> beings who will nourish and respect us.
>
> —*Popul Vuh*

Writing this off as "merely mythology" may create a seemingly safe
certainty. However, it also keeps humans in a state of denial about
what really happened to them in the past. Could it be that we turned
out to be more intelligent than our creators? Is it possible that we were
brutally treated because we refused to act like domesticated beasts of
burden? According to the *Popul Vuh,* the dumbing down worked (in
this case after five previous, ineffective experiments). What exactly
was it that they were trying to dumb down?

> They saw and they instantly could see far,
> they succeeded in seeing, they succeeded in
> knowing where all is in the world. When they
> looked, they saw instantly all around them,
> and they contemplated in turn the arch of the
> heaven and the round face of the earth.
>
> —*Popul Vuh*

This is what had to be dumbed down. This is what frightened
our creators. This was one of the most heinous acts of our misguided
creators. We were genetically engineered and conditioned from birth
to be creatures that would venerate and worship those who "created"—and spiritually raped—us. The *Popul Vuh* states how the gods
were finally "victorious" in making us obedient workers who worshipped our genetic creators as if they were the creators of the universe
and the creators of the soul.

In actuality, they were liars who were bored and used us as play
fodder. They demanded worship because their souls were undevel-
oped. They made us fight their wars because they lacked the resolve
and courage to fight them on their own. They made us build large edi-
fices to praise them when they weren't even close to being worthy of
our praise. We believed all of this because we had been so dumbed

down that we no longer had the capacity to question those who committed this spiritual tyranny. We worshipped them because they treated us quite brutally if we didn't. We fought their wars because we knew that we would be slaughtered if we didn't. We praised them because that was what they wanted, and they got quite nasty if they didn't get their way.

With every veneration and praise, we etched the cellular conditioning that these pretenders were God. We must have known that this was a sham because we resisted valiantly. Jehovah kept the Israelites in the wilderness for forty years so that he could have a third generation of killer warriors. He didn't want a complaining Moses, nor a questioning Aaron. After forty years he had Joshua who moved—and destroyed—without question. The violation of another people's sovereignty wasn't even questioned. Pretender god Jehovah ordained it, and the highly conditioned Israelites marched forward in their slaughter.

In the *Bhagavad Gita,* the warrior Arjuna wants to work out a peace with his enemies. However, Krishna at first persuades and then eventually goads Arjuna into fighting. How amazing that very few people are willing to see Krishna as the warmonger and Arjuna as the willing peacemaker. Because Krishna is seen as a God, most who read this account figure that he must have been right.

He wasn't. He was a technologically advanced being who was only interested in overcoming boredom and conquering territory. He didn't care the slightest bit about the development of Arjuna's soul.

One only need look as far as the *Old Testament* to see an example of a god meddling in the process of peacemaking. Moses and Pharaoh had worked out a separate peace, but Jehovah would have none of it. He wanted slaughter—and most likely good theater. He wanted it so badly that he told Moses that he (Jehovah) had hardened Pharaoh's heart so that he might do battle. This, of course, led to the Red Sea slaughter that, according to one of David's Psalms, killed many on both sides. Yet Moses and Pharaoh had worked it out so this would have to happen. Jehovah probably needed a way to get his Israelites into the desert so that he could whip them into shape and make sure that no peacemakers ever messed with his plans again.

This is rape—spiritual and physical. The conditioning has etched itself so deeply into our cellular memory that the slaughtering by the Serbs in Bosnia and the outrageous genocide in Darfur, Sudan seem more like natural reflexes than horrific acts. The massacre of 6,000,000 Jews was an easy process. The Christians in the area smelled the bodies burning, but they could not or would not resist. This comes as much from war conditioning as slave conditioning.

These "wonderful" gods beat us into submission if we dared to move out of our "slave chip" paradigm. 5,000 years later, when the escape from the Sobibor concentration camp began (with most of the SS officers already killed), many could not run to their freedom. Many simply stood with heads bowed and prayed instead of running. Now that's powerful conditioning—conditioning that began 5,000 to 10,000 years ago and continues today like a slave chip playing repeatedly in our brains.

What could they do to us then that caused us to be like this now?

## AN OFFER YOU BETTER NOT REFUSE

### Jehovah's Devastating Covenant

Anyone reading Jehovah's words out of the context of the *Old Testament* would conclude that these were either the words of a raving lunatic or the ramblings of someone no longer grounded in reality.

> If you follow my laws and faithfully observe
> my commandments, I will grant you rains
> in their season so that the earth shall yield
> its produce and the trees of the field their

fruit. Your threshing shall overtake the vintage,
and the vintage shall overtake the sowing;
you shall eat your fill of bread and dwell
securely in your land.

I will grant peace in the land, and you will
lie down untroubled by anyone; I will give the
land respite from vicious beasts, and no sword
shall cross your land. You shall give chase to
your enemies, and they shall fall before you by
the sword...

I will look with favor upon you, and make you
fertile and multiply you; and I will maintain
my covenant with you. You shall eat grain
long stored...

(Leviticus 26:3-10)

These are the words of Yahweh/Jehovah to the Israelites. Sounds like a fair deal... right? Think for a moment about this. Consider that you own a thriving business; you are doing quite well on your own business initiative. In comes a well-dressed character and says, "I have a deal for you. If you will pay me $3,000 a month, I will make sure that your business continues to be successful."

You mention that your business is doing quite well on its own and that you don't need help from anyone.

Then the man leans closer to you and says, "You don't under-stand. If you don't pay us the $3,000 each month, we're going to stand outside your door and tell people that we've been cheated. We're going to tell people that you won't honor your commitments and that your merchandise will break down within weeks. We're going to tell people that you're planning to go out of business and that your customers will be stuck with your product."

Immediately, you recognize the protection racket. These people are simply protecting you from the wrath that they intend to wreak upon you. You are gaining nothing, but instead have to pay for things to remain the same.

What does this have to do with Jehovah? Read on:

> But if you do not obey me and do not observe
> these commandments, if you reject my laws and
> spurn my norms, so that you do not observe
> all of my commandments and you break my
> Covenant, I in turn will do this to you. I will
> wreak misery upon you—consumption and fever,
> which cause the eyes to pine and the body to
> languish; you shall sow your seed to no purpose,
> for your enemies shall eat it. I will set my face
> against you; you shall be routed by your enemies,
> and your foes shall dominate you. You shall flee
> though none pursues.
>
> (Leviticus 26:14-17)

This is not a loving God who cares for his children. This is instead a highly manipulative warlord claiming to be God—a pretender to the throne. This is a petty entity, incapable of gentle persuasion, who is spiritually raping the people he claims to love.

But hang on, it gets "better":

> And if for all that you do not obey me, I will
> go on disciplining you sevenfold for your sins,
> and I will break your proud glory. I will make
> the skies like iron and your earth like copper,
> so that your strength shall be spent to no
> purpose. Your land shall not yield its produce,
> nor shall the trees of it yield their fruit.
>
> (Leviticus 26:18-20)

Sevenfold for your sins... isn't that a bit excessive? What happened to an eye for an eye? This is seven days of detention for an offense requiring one day. This is swatting a dog on seven different occasions for defecating once on the rug. Plain and simply put, this is cruel and unusual punishment—the kind of punishment meted out by vengeful people set on effecting a vendetta. Yet few—even in the Mafia—would mete out a seven-fold vendetta. This is the pronouncement of a very sick mind. Yet Jehovah told the Israelites that he was God—the only God worthy of being worshipped. By his very actions this pretender god was worthy of nothing but our contempt.

However, this "deal" that Jehovah is forcing on his people gets even worse:

> And if for all that, you do not obey me,
> I will go on disciplining you seven fold
> for your sins. I will loose wild beasts
> against you, and they shall bereave you
> of your children, and wipe out your cattle...
>
> ...and if you withdraw into your cities, I
> will send pestilence among you, and you
> shall be delivered into enemy hands....
> You shall eat the flesh of your sons and
> the flesh of your daughters.... I will heap
> your carcasses on your lifeless fetishes.
>
> I will spurn you. I will lay your cities in
> ruin and make your sanctuaries desolate....
> And you will scatter among nations, and I
> will unsheathe the sword against you. Your
> land shall become a desolation and your
> cities a ruin.
>
> (Leviticus 26:21-33)

Christian O'Brien, author of *The Genius of the Few,* claims that this covenant was disturbing for four reasons: (1) it was not a freely negotiated agreement between both parties; (2) the punishments proposed were not even close to being civilized; (3) people other than the offenders would be punished—the good would have to suffer along with the bad; (4) sin was being returned with evil—the punishment went far beyond the elements of the "crime."

However, understanding the dark side of Jehovah is essential. This is the entity who ordered a man stoned to death for picking up sticks on the Sabbath. This is the entity who threw poisonous snakes into a crowd of people—and killed many of them—simply because they were complaining. This is the entity who beamed with joy when he was told that one of his follower had impaled someone because he was not following the commandments.

This is also the entity who—despite claiming to be omnipotent—warned only a few people of an impending natural disaster and watched from above as millions of his creations died a terrifying death by drowning. This is the entity that a majority of Americans worship as the God of the Christians and Jews.

This is also the god who spiritually raped us—his new creations—and created a past shock that lies deep within each and every one of us. This is the entity who insured that we would continue to worship him long after he departed. Exactly how did he do that? He and his cohorts designed a system of conditioning so effective that its devastating impact remains even today. What these pretender gods created in order to keep us in line was religion.

## THE ORIGINS OF RELIGION

### Conditioning the New Creations to Be Spiritual Slaves

For just a couple of minutes, assume that you are very high up in the ranks of these pretender gods. You created humans as a slave race—a herd to do your dirty work. With extended leisure time, you decided that you needed some warriors to help you conquer lands from the other entities that were mining the planet. When these chess-like battles became boring, you decided that you needed some entertainment—something more like theater.

But for now, the warriors are refusing to fight—or play their proper roles. The workers are refusing to work and are expending their energies, instead, in rioting. Also—God forbid—many who are realizing that their lives don't show much promise are committing suicide. Just how do you make sure that your new creations fight your wars, do your dirty work, and stop committing suicide? After much discussion among the ranks, you finally come to an answer: create a religion.

In this religion you promise rewards in the next life—for eternity—as long as your creations play *your* game in this life. Not theirs. This means sweating and toiling without rebellion. It also means worshipping those who created you. For those who are just a tad unimpressed, you invent another place called Hell, which promises great misery for eternity if your laws are not kept. To insure that they continue fighting for you, you promise that dying in war is an automatic ticket to heaven.

Additionally, those who commit suicide automatically go to hell. This insures that those humans who get depressed with their lot will remain with that lot, stuck fast in the hope that they will get to rest for eternity. In an attempt to secure an eternity in Paradise, these badly conditioned and spiritually raped humans will spend their free time worshipping the creators and bending to their every whim. Because they have successfully blocked any memory of the spiritual realms—and all memory of past lives—these newly created humans have no way to prove whether this religion is real or false. Since religion deals in eternities, one quickly realizes that it is best to play the game of the pretender gods.

Being one of these pretender gods, you had to be rock sure that your creations played your game according to your rules. To achieve this surety, you create the ultimate cosmic "good cop\bad cop" game.

You construct a personal embodiment of a force that is trying to keep your creations in a state of sin (wanting to worship other gods, not obeying the dictates of the gods, not wanting to work, lusting after other women, etc.). You claim that this other entity wants their souls and that, if this entity succeeds, they will spend all of eternity in hell. Thus, when you are told by one of these humans that he feels he is being exploited or that he wants to make peace with his enemies, you can tell him that this is the evil one working in his life. He should pray to be guided by the forces of righteousness (that being you).

What is interesting in all this is that when any of your rebellious forces experience pangs of conscience for what you are doing to them, you can condition them into believing that those who want to liberate them are evil. This is what happened with the Serpent in the Garden of Eden. This is what happened with Prometheus when he stole fire from the gods and gave it to humanity. This is what happened with the Norse god Loki who tried to throw a "monkey wrench" into the slave conditioning of the gods and, according to the legend, made things so unbearable for them that they finally left.

The pretender gods themselves may have left, but their conditioning remains. Inside each and every one of us is a slave chip that continues the conditioning of these despicable beings. This slave chip is the result of many genetic experiments and thousands of years of religious conditioning. We follow that conditioning today as if these pretender gods were still in our midst. The singer of the song might be gone, but the melody lingers on with a devastating impact.

During the Korean War a soldier was told to guard a certain area until he was relieved. However, unbeknownst to the soldier, during his time at post the enemy had wiped out the squad he was guarding. Thus, for three days he continued to guard the area. Finally, sometime into the fourth day he collapsed from exhaustion and slept. When he woke up, he felt tremendous guilt that he had fallen asleep. He had no way of knowing that no one could have possibly relieved him. So he continued in his guilt, believing that it was his fault that all of his squadron was killed.

Humanity is collectively like that soldier. As early humans, we were conditioned to worship interlopers and pretenders as God. These pretenders deserted us and left us to our own resources to survive because they no longer had need of us. However, that awesome and devastating conditioning remains with us, and we stay at our "post". Like sheep, we continue the patterns of worship. We still offer our bodies to fight the holy wars—and have hopes of paradise for participating in the slaughter.

Our world of work is still not structured to serve the worker; instead, god-like "superiors" are paid much more than they are worth because they can easily find worker drones who will work for much less than they are worth. We are so well conditioned that most any movement toward spiritual liberation will create guilt and a feeling that one is falling from the fold. We have been programmed well. We feel spiritually nourished to the degree that we remain as spiritual slaves.

With no guidance from the pretender gods—or God himself, we burned brilliant people like John Hus and Giordano Bruno at the stake, threatened Galileo with brutal torture, and were able to free captured hostages from the embassy of "The Great Satan" in Iran. All in the name of Christ, humans have slaughtered whole cities, raped and massacred the Indians we were trying to convert, and held heresy trails and painful executions for those who dared not believe. We continue to sing praises to a long gone force "which saved a wretch like me." We see ourselves as sin-bound creatures. Those who "refuse" to see in such a light still suffer from the dumbing down of the pretender gods. We walk this planet with a brain that is capable of moving mountains, yet we still use very little of it.

We are victims of a long-past spiritual rape that had made past shock a part of our experience. The more we are willing to face what actually happened in our past, the more that we will be able to overcome this past shock and begin living as the humans that we are capable of becoming. The time to begin this exploration is now.

# APPENDIX B

# Spiritual Autobiography
# From Believer to Explorer

## The Path from Conditioning towards the Truth

My publisher and I discussed putting an addendum to this book. Coming up in the discussion was the consideration of putting in a biographical account of the events in my life that took me from being a devout born again Christian to the spiritual warrior and explorer that I am today. I resisted this, thinking it was vain and self-serving. I had already protested having my picture on the book, and had given in to that request. However, I also realized that my journey has been both unique and universal.

My journey is unique because, comparatively speaking, few have questioned and deeply researched the belief systems that they were brought up on. Consensus reality is powerful, and most do not want to stray outside of it. However, my journey is becoming increasingly universal. Now, exponentially increasing numbers of well-meaning people are beginning to question the consensus reality of what they had been assured was "God's truth."

I now realize that the times I thought I was the most "deranged" were when I was closest to the truth. The times that my conditioning assured me that I was falling from the grace of God were actually when I was closest to God. At those times that I was almost completely sure that I was an immature rebel, I was, instead, closest to the truth about God.

I promised my publisher (and myself) that I would send him material only if I found it compelling and nourishing to the soul who is searching for truth. As I wrote this material, I realized that this was the first time in my life that I had organized and recorded thoughts about my life. The experience was liberating, fulfilling, and revealing. As I used the computerized outline program I could push a button and see only the main headings of my life. Pushing another button revealed those headings and all the details of a spiritual journey, which still has not reached its destination. Yet with this emerging eagle's eye view of my life, I sensed that something very powerful had been guiding me.

My new age friends told me that it was my higher self, something deep within me that is at a higher level of consciousness. My Christian friends assured me that this leading had to come from Jesus Christ himself. Other hybrids, caught between the Christian and new age spectrum, assured me that the Holy Spirit was guiding me. The atheists and agnostics figured I was making all of this up in my head, but did agree that I had had a most vivid and meaningful life. My take is that I don't care who or what it is, but I am fairly sure that it has something to do with whatever force keeps us linked to the true God.

Whatever force that is, labels mean nothing. What impresses me is its wisdom and guidance. While I would have preferred a burning bush or a parting of the Red Sea thrown in once in a while to ease the confusion, I also admit with great humility that I have probably had hundreds of them and just wasn't paying attention.

What caused me to finally submit this autobiography to my publisher was much deeper than his compelling request. It was something universal. Others with a more narrow view all over this world are starting to feel the religious stirrings that I felt in my early teen years. Still others who are positive that their passion for truth is resulting from the devil's leading, may discover as they read on that these passions for truth may actually be coming from God, the true God. Those who feel guilty because they choose to explore a different path might just realize that the path they are walking is a limb that gets thicker as one walks back to the trunk of the tree. This biography is written for those who have this gnawing inside of them that something is wrong. I had it for years, and feared that I would burn in hell if I succumbed to exploring research that pointed out that what we have been told as children is not the truth.

If this short biography makes any spiritual explorer feel less alone and helps deepen that passion to *know*, then this reliving of my past will have done its job.

## INTRODUCTION [1937-1950]

Nothing is more devastating to a child than having his parents tell him or her what the truth is about God. The child's capacity for experiencing God is pristine. Children actually have a much greater chance of experiencing God than their parents. They have not yet been brainwashed. They have no programming to guide them along the severely brainwashed reality tunnels of their parents. Without any verbal prodding, they can experience God at deep levels.

Then shades of the religious prison house are thrust upon the child. The child believes in the authority of his parents. For the moment, the parents are perceived as God's representatives. They are adults. They know. How can they be wrong?

But they are. All they are passing along to their children is the brainwashing that had been passed along to them by their parents. Trace it back far enough and one comes to the pretender gods, conditioning their newly formed humans to believe that they were God. The past becomes prologue to a drama. It stifles experience and embraces belief.

That is what happens to everyone.

That is what happened to me.

My parents were good people. They meant well. To allow me to come to conclusions on my own about God would have been blasphemy. From their very well established paradigm, this would have been putting my mortal soul in danger. They "did the right thing." They passed on to me the conditioning of the pretender gods.

## GETTING SAVED  [1950]

I have read dozens of papers from my composition students that inform me that the day they accepted Jesus Christ as their Lord and Savior was the best day of their life. For me, the day was November 8, 1950. I was 13, full of raging hormones, and the major cause of stress for both of my parents. I got in trouble at school, had already failed seventh grade, and was failing four out of five subjects in eighth grade. During the bus ride to school, I was often the prime target of bullies and others who needed a ready scapegoat to compensate for their ailing loss of self-esteem. Worst of all, I wasn't having any luck impressing the girls.

I was a prime candidate for "salvation."

One day I had managed to offend a whole portion of the neighborhood by letting loose with a salvo of profanity the likes of which had never been heard there before. I was being tied up, beaten up, my face was bleeding in three places, and I figured all I had left was the power of words. (I was soon to be a professional writer, so the idea must have had some merit.) Charlie Stricklin was the main offender, ramming something into my mouth and cutting my lip. That's when I let roar:

Cut it out you God damn f***ing sons of bitches!

Mrs. Stricklin, an activist for Christ if there ever was one, came quickly onto the scene. I was positive that God was sending her to rescue me. Instead she grabbed me by the hair and very loudly castigated me for taking her Lord's name in vain. I informed her in the most immature manner possible that it was her f***ing son who was beating up on someone who couldn't defend himself, and that sure as hell wasn't very Christ-like. Her glaring look caused me to feel such guilt. Somehow I believed her when she told me that God was punishing me.

Then she let loose with the corker. If I had Jesus in my heart, I would find it impossible to use language like I had just used. Mrs. Stricklin was a real crusader. She was leading a neighborhood campaign to get my minister thrown out of his church. She was God's mighty pain in the ass—a role that I would eventually assume at the youth level. Her mission now was to get me to a Jack Wyrtzen rally and get my ass saved. It was arranged.

On the ride to the rally Mrs. Stricklin made it clear that if a truck plowed into the car and killed all six of us, five of the six would go immediately to heaven, and my posterior would be roasting on a spit. In his address, Jack Wyrtzen reinforced the heat imagery. After assuring the fold that Buddha, Mohammed, and other religious leaders were roasting in hell, he came up with what I now refer to in my English classes as a rousing metaphor. He claimed that hell would be so hot that molten lead would taste like an ice cream cone. I'll say one thing for old Jack: he sure picked some powerful imagery.

When the altar call came, I was one of the first to go forward. At the time I was sure that I was getting eternal fire insurance. What I realize now is that Jack Wyrtzen and many other evangelists knew how to tap into the pretender gods' conditioning archetypes. What appeared to be salvation was instead an archetype induced catharsis. Sadly, Carl Gustav Jung wasn't on hand to explain that to me.

## WATCHING "FIRE UPON THE EARTH" [1950]

When I was 13 years old, I would have to attend church twice on Sundays, once in the morning and once in the evening. My church, Covenant Methodist Church, had the practice of showing movies for the evening service. Most of these were awful films. One that vividly stands out in my mind is the story of a young boy who breaks one of the stained glass windows of a neighboring church. No one ever finds out who did it until twenty years later. In the final scene of the film, this young minister is standing in the pulpit, tears running down his face. He confesses that he was the boy who broke the glass long, long ago. The congregation begins crying along with the minister as he states how God's grace let him know that he could be forgiven for anything. Tears of joy were streaming down my face as I realized that this probably meant that the film was finally coming to an end.

On an October night in 1950, I went to the evening service prepared to endure an hour of boredom. The film for that evening was called *Fire upon the Earth* and portrayed the role of the Protestant Reformation. For about twenty minutes it appeared that my expectations of boredom would be fulfilled. However, when the film came to the account of the Czechoslovakian reformer John Hus, I found myself sitting forward in rapt attention. Both of my parents looked at me, surprised because they rarely saw me being attentive to much of anything. I had failed seventh grade the year before, and in another year and a half, I would fail ninth grade. But there was something about the life of John Hus portrayed on the screen that gripped me deeply. I was choking back tears as I watched the pictures of an artist's rendition of Hus being burned at the stake.

John Hus was a priest in the late 14th century who wanted the Bible translated into Czech, the language of his people. The Vatican told him that this would be blasphemy. He was aware of John Wycliffe's increasing success in translating the Bible into English. Support began to swell around Hus. Other priests like Jerome of Prague, as well as common people, joined Hus in his quest. These people were eventually called Hussites. In 1415 Hus were burned at the stake, despite successfully defending himself against 33 charges of heresy.

As I watched the events of this low budget film unfold on the screen, I began shaking and had to choke back tears. To me, this was one of the bravest acts in history. But it was something deeper than that, and it would take me years to understand it.

## DENMARK [1964-1965]

Living, teaching, and studying in Denmark probably represented the best year in my life. For that year I answered to no one. Before spending six months at a Danish Folk School, I lived for two one month periods with two different families, both generously giving of their time to teach me Danish. Of course, I fell in love with a Danish girl who spoke perfect English and didn't want to struggle with my jumbled Danish. After the Danish school session, I traveled the European continent not knowing where my next stop or meal would be. I left the United States in August of 1964 with $1800 in travelers cheques. I returned in August of 1965 with $18.

The value of the year was that I had experienced a sense of freedom in Europe as an alternative to becoming head of the English Department at the high school where I had been teaching. For a year I was relatively free of conditioning and paradigms. My conditioned consensus reality simply did not play in Denmark.

But I was still in the Christian mold, despite the fact that I was away from the conditioning. Danes are highly irreverent people who tolerate religion much more than they embrace it. They are not the conditioned people that Americans are. Causing a Dane to feel guilty about something relating to God would be a laborious task. Being that I was planning to marry this delightful Danish woman, I felt that she should be brought into the fold, so I took her to see Billy Graham during his 1965 Denmark Crusade. Ulla responded to the altar call and became very involved in Denmark's ultra-fundamentalist Indremission Church. What she never responded to was my pleading that she come to the United States.

## TRIP TO PRAGUE [1967]

In the summer of 1967 I was in charge of a group of 28 students studying German in Salzburg. This was a six-week program and I had three days of vacation coming up, my only break for the entire program. I wanted to go to Budapest because I had been teaching James Michener's *The Bridge at Andau*. This is a stirring account of the Hungarian Revolution of 1956. My intention was to take slides that I could show my students.

I asked if I could have an additional three days to go to Prague, and was told that would be no problem. However, a late arriving Visa prevented my departure with two friends, and I ended up in Prague alone with the worst strep throat of my life. In Vienna the pain was so bad that I seriously considered waiting in Vienna until I met up with my friends on their way to Budapest. Yet something deep inside me drove me to make the train journey to Prague.

I got off the train realizing that I would never connect with my friends. I was in Czechoslovakia one year before the Russian crackdown, and the people I was supposed to stay with were not at the train station. With the pain and lonely circumstances I was sure this was the worst day of my life. Little did I realize that this would turn out to be one of the most amazing.

The amazement started with my decision not to turn around and get back on the train to Vienna. Paralyzed by the communist fear of the time, I grabbed my suitcase and began walking around the city. For reasons I cannot to this day understand, I walked across the Valtva River and walked for two or three miles around the city of Prague, all of this time carrying a heavy suitcase. When I came in the vicinity of the Prince Charles Church, I began feeling so uneasy that I forgot that I was sick.

I began "recognizing" my surroundings. In a sort of déjà vu, I was able to sense the distinction of what was new to the area and what was still around from the turn of the 14th century. I also "knew" the way to the Prince Charles Church and began walking in that direction. At this point in my life I was a fundamentalist Christian and any ideas of past life recall or reincarnation were not part of my paradigm. That did not stop me from knowing exactly where to go.

Being a good Christian, I went home and shut all of this out.

## READING ABOUT JOHN HUS IN SEMINARY [1968]

About the third week of my first semester at Gordon-Conwell Theological Institute, I found myself with a most interesting assignment in Church History. Professor Kerr wanted us to do hundreds of pages of outside reading and, remembering my experience in Prague, I chose to read more deeply about John Hus.

I had told absolutely no one about my déjà vu experience in Prague. Not only was I sure that others would think I was crazy, but I was fairly sure that I was crazy myself. Well, not exactly crazy — just being tricked by the Devil. That's the way my mind worked then. If something strayed outside of the spiritually correct paradigm, it had to be the Devil. Later on, I would constantly remark to fellow students: "This Devil is really something; he appears to have more power than God himself." However, during my first year at seminary I was elected president of my class, and for about half of my first semester I was actually successful in not rocking the boat.

That was until I started reading about John Hus and his friend Jerome of Prague. Neither of these Czech reformers were spiritually correct in the eyes of Christiandom. They stood up against the Vatican powers that be, and garnered a following that insisted that the Roman Catholic Church reform. This was nearly 140 years before Martin Luther tacked his 95 Theses on the Wittenberg church door. Both John and Jerome were priests and used the power of the Bible itself to advance their arguments. They debated, created a passion for reformation, and were eventually burned at the stake to "exorcise" their ideas. Yet after their deaths the Hussite movement continued for another thirty years.

The film that had introduced me to John Hus eighteen years previously was called *Fire Upon the Earth*. I was now reading seven books about Hus that were creating a fire in my soul. I began discussing with both my fellow students and professors the idea that the Protestant Church needed a reformation just like the Catholic Church of old. With the greatest of irony, many of my professors agreed, yet the students felt this was a bad idea.

At night I would have long discussions with my wife Mary concerning the discoveries I was making about this little known pocket of resistance led by John Hus.

## KONSTANZ [1970]

The first real crack in my Christian shell came during a drive to Zurich. I was still officially in seminary, but I had persuaded the school to give me a semester's credit for traveling in Europe and visiting the Holy Land. I had four separate projects for which I would receive a total of 16 credit hours. Mary and I were on the way to the L'Abri fellowship in Switzerland. We were having the time of our lives going from city to city, attending a different opera every night. It didn't matter what the city was as long as it had an opera we both wanted to see.

The night before, in a small German city, we had seen Mozart's *Magic Flute*. Now we were driving to Zurich to see Verdi's *A Masked Ball*. I asked Mary if we could get up early so that we could make a side trip to Konstanz. Mary knew that this town meant a lot to me because this is where John Hus and Jerome of Prague were burned at the stake. Konstanz required an extra seventy miles driving, and we arrived in the early afternoon.

As soon as I got out of the car in Konstanz, I had a déjà vu of my previous déjà vu—something that I had repressed for three years simply because I could not understand it. Now the experience in Prague was overwhelming me. While I had never shared my déjà vu Prague experience with my wife, she was now sharing my confusion. She knew I was in a strange state. Trying to break the trance, she suggested that we get a map and find the Hussenstein, the stone marking the spot where Hus, Jerome, and many other Hussites were burned at the stake.

My claiming that I didn't need a map was no surprise to Mary. I was one of those male types who would rather die than ask for directions. But I did not need directions because "I knew where I was." Without ever having been there, I walked a straight line to the town square where the Hussenstein was located. As soon as I came into the square, I immediately looked in the direction of the stone. I did my best to keep this from Mary, but sensed that she could feel my "out of the paradigm" confusion. I walked over to the stone and just stared at it. For a few moments I wasn't even aware that I was married and had my wife with me. The feelings that I had inside were powerful and totally strange to me, much more powerful than anything I had experienced in Prague. We were supposed to get something to eat, but I was feeling no pangs of hunger.

What I was feeling was awareness and remembrance.

## APOTHESIS

Seminary was agony for me despite the faculty consisting of very good people who seemed to understand what I was going through. I was moving from being a born again Christian who was studying to preach the Gospel to becoming a heretic who, at the moment, was reading about a Christian heresy called Gnosticism. I also began writing seriously and had one of my poems and two of my short stories selected for publication. I began writing articles for magazines.

The magazine that I have written the most articles for is *New Perspectives*. Its editor, Alan Hartley, was the first to put a picture of me on the cover of his magazine, and as of this writing he is still the only one to bestow that honor on me. I wrote 22 articles for *New Perspectives*. Only a couple of articles didn't work out. It was the research for one of these articles which significantly impacted my life.

Alan and I had discussed doing one or two articles on the subject of past life therapy. He felt that I would be a good person to do this article. Despite my experiences in Prague, Konstanz, and seminary, I still wasn't sure whether reincarnation was a reality. Despite these doubts, I had talked to many people who felt that past life therapy had a very positive effect on their healing.

For those who do not fully understand past life therapy, its main tenet is that problems—physical and mental—may be the result of what someone experienced in a previous life. If one has an intense fear of fire, perhaps he had burned to death in a previous life. If a man has a fear of intimacy with women, it might be because he had a bad experience with a woman in a previous life. If a person is having an inexplicable pain in a certain part of her body, that pain might be the result of a severe wound received in a previous life. I would not have taken much of this seriously except for the volumes of cases that had responded effectively to past life therapy. My take was, maybe it was reincarnation, maybe it was a very effective metaphor. If the person was healed, who cares?

Thus, I decided to do what I had done in more than two-thirds of my articles—become involved in the process and then write about it. I made the decision to have one session each with past life therapists in San Diego, Sacramento, and San Jose. The sessions were so revealing that I ended up having three sessions each with two of the therapists, and eight sessions with the third. What I experienced with three therapists was so powerful that I realized that I no longer had the objectivity to write an article. The process became more important than the research.

My first session was with a woman named Trish. Trish did past life therapy with a unique twist. She did deep tissue massage and got her impressions from what she felt in the body. Ten minutes into the session she sensed great muscle tension in my shoulder area. Of course she massaged it deeply, and I screamed bloody murder. What she said while she was doing this rocked me:

> You have a lot of terror locked up in this area of your
> body. I think your body is tight because you are

being burned at the stake. You have been tried for heresy and you are brutally tied to the stake. I sense that this is happening in Western Europe, but that is not your home. Your home is in either Czechoslovakia or Poland. You are one of the leaders of a religious reform movement and the church is very angry with you.

I wanted to say something, but I remained the objective journalist and said nothing that would guide or lead her.

A lot of what is happening in your life today is influenced by this brutal death. You are terrified of being burned at the stake again. You are afraid to write the books that you really want to write because something deep inside of you fears going to hell.

She hit it right on the head. I had stopped cold with my writing—especially books like *Past Shock.* I stopped writing for fourteen months and didn't look at or do any work with the manuscript. I had this heavy feeling that I was committing blasphemy and would be punished severely—even if it wasn't being burned at the stake.

As amazing as this experience was, I tried to put it out of my mind. I had an article to write and two more past life therapists to have sessions with.

Art was the second past life therapist. He did not do massage, but he did touch certain parts of the body in order to get his impressions. When he touched the very same spot that Trish touched, I once again let out a yelp. His impressions frighteningly corresponded with Trish's:

You have an irrational fear of going to hell. You experienced something very traumatic sometime in the thirteen or fourteen hundreds. This was in

Eastern Europe. I get the impression that you got a foretaste of hell by being burned at the stake. You made a lot of people angry and they got you good. These people can't hurt you now. You can't be burned at the stake anymore, and God isn't going to send you to hell for attempting to tell the truth. Even if you are wrong, God is not going to send you to hell. But you're carrying a lot of baggage from that lifetime. Your death was so traumatic that is impacting decisions you are making today. I want to help you get beyond that.

Being burned at the stake truly is not much fun. John Hus's final images as he writhed in pain were of people coming up to the fire and throwing branches on it to make it burn better. It is a slow, painful death. Millions of people from the Dark Ages up to the Renaissance died in this horrendously slow way. Some estimates claim that more than five million innocent people were put to death in various ways simply because they had the wrong beliefs. This is not a legacy that any Christian can be proud of. Yet when I was in seminary, I heard some calls for bringing back heresy trials. But we have made some progress: None suggested that we burn people at the stake.

You might find this hard to believe, but I was not that impressed with seminary. In my classes I spoke out and mentioned how the Catholic Church had to get rid of all existing references to reincarnation in the early 6th Century because the idea of getting a second chance for salvation took away the element of control from the Church. (Good heavens, a person might come back as a Buddhist and decide that he liked that better.) Getting many chances to spiritually grow and evolve through reincarnation just didn't sit well with church leaders who thought their particular dogma was the only way to gain eternal life. For those students who became adamant that each soul got only one shot at the heavenly experience, I said that that is exactly what they had believed for the past five lifetimes. This was meant to be funny, but few laughed. Many said they would pray for me. And all of this information was coming from someone (me) who wasn't even sure if reincarnation was a reality.

What rocked that questioning paradigm of mine was my past life reading from a woman named Kirin in San Diego. Kirin immediately picked up on my wrist and back pain and told me that the pain went back to when I was tied very tightly to a stake, right before I was burned to death.

This was the point where my paradigm began coming apart. The previous two past life readers I visited said almost the same identical things.

Then she stated something that really rocked me:

> I'm getting a very strong impression of you walking across a bridge. I think this bridge is in what used to be Czechoslovakia. This is a long bridge and you are terrified of the storm, but even more terrified of the priest who is going to be angry with you because you are an altar boy and you are late for mass.

I immediately imagined the wide Valtva River that ran through both sections of the city of Prague. I sensed that the church was the Prince Charles Church because this was the church that I walked to in 1967 when I had that powerful déjà vu experience. But I forced myself to listen:

> You are 14 years old, and the priest really frightens you. He has this horrible breath that makes you sick. He is a decaying and dying man, yet you must please him because you know that you want to become a priest, and if you don't please this man, this will be impossible. Your parents are pressuring you to be a priest. You agree with them because you want to serve God.

I was fighting hard, as a journalist, not to say anything that would guide or lead Kirin. It was at this moment that I sensed I would probably never write an article about past life therapy because my objectivity was gone. I wanted to know more.

> You became a priest, but you joined up with some people who were quite threatening to the church. These people wanted regular church members to have more freedom about what they did with their lives. Most of these people were burned at the stake.

Kirin then asked me if I had recently experienced pneumonia. I told her that yes, I had it twice in a one-year period, and it struck me as strange because I was usually a very healthy person. I could not understand why I would get that sick. Kirin had an explanation.

> You were in prison for more than a year. It was in extremely unhealthy conditions. You froze in the winter and were in a hot, moldy environment in summer. You suffered from pneumonia for most of that year. If you hadn't been burned at the stake, you would have soon died from pneumonia. Your two bouts with pneumonia have nothing to do with anything in this lifetime. This was a cleansing and a final releasing of that which you had experienced before.

For a cleansing, it sure wasn't fun. During the second bout, I experienced a three day period in which I was fairly sure that I was going to die, and was so miserable that I was almost okay with it.

Kirin had given me a lot to think about, but her insights kept coming:

> This past life of yours has impacted this lifetime, in good and bad ways. The good is that you and those you were leading did not give

up. You died for what you believed in.
However, as you were dying, you had doubts
about whether you had done the right thing in
your life. The people who were tying you to
the stake wanted to inflict great amounts of
pain on you. They tied the ropes around you so
tight that you could barely breathe. You were
in so much pain that you almost welcomed the
flames. As the flames were leaping around
you, people were cheering because one of the
big leaders of the heretics was finally having
his life ended in a very painful manner. Your
mission and passion in life was and is to free
people from religious oppression. It's a divine
mission, but it is a dangerous one. Freeing
people from religious oppression is why you
came into this present lifetime.

Is any of this valid? I don't know. I do know that I can no
longer dismiss this as mere coincidence.

Was I John Hus? I still have doubts. I am driven crazy by people who tell me that they were someone famous in a previous life. I
have yet to meet someone who spent a previous life simply shoveling
cow dung in Lithuania. If one third of the past life readers (as opposed
to past life therapists) are correct in their assessments, we have at least
300,000 people in America who were one of the twelve disciples, and
only one has claimed to be Judas. (This being the great writer of *The
Prophet*, Kahil Gibran.) We have at least 50,000 Virgin Marys, and this
is just in the United States.

Was I a leader of the Hussite movement? I don't know and I
don't really care. I am now Jack Barranger, a teacher and writer who
wants to contribute to people's personal and spiritual freedom. I feel a
kinship with Jerome of Prague. He was a very tall man, and so am I.
His final words are stirring:

Light the fire before my face. If I were afraid
of death, I would not have come here.

Whether I was Judas, a farmer shoveling dung in Lithuania, or
a heretic follower of John Hus doesn't really matter. What does matter
is the kinship I feel with Jerome. I sense that he was terrified beyond
belief when he stated those brave words. If I indeed had pneumonia as
a Hussite in 1415, re-experiencing it in 1995 was a real pain in the ass.
If reincarnation is real, I want to meet with the committee in charge
and make some suggestions:

> Hey, folks, I damn near died in the
> summer of 1995 and I wasn't having
> any fun. Somehow I missed the spiri-
> tual value of this.

In 1996 I had a third session with Kirin. Nothing about Prague
or the Hussites came up. In a way I was disappointed. However, Kirin
came up with a lifetime in the Crusades that struck me with such force
that I was stunned:

> You joined the Crusades early in their move-
> ment. You were excited and felt that you were
> performing God's will. However, you watched
> the decay and corruption and it reduced you to
> tears every day. You observed live babies
> being roasted over an open fire and men eating
> the roasted flesh. You watched your close
> friends raping women repeatedly and killing
> the women when they were done with them.
> These were married men, and you were the
> strange one because you remained faithful to
> your wife and four children. You saw men
> melting lead and pouring it on the faces of
> screaming children. You were horrified, and
> when you expressed your horror, the leaders
> claimed that you were sinning against God.

Kirin claimed that she knew little to nothing about the Crusades, yet to the details mentioned above, and others that she mentioned, were amazingly accurate. What convinced me more than the words was the pain I was experiencing as she recounted this. This was real—more real than anything I had experienced in any of my past life sessions.

Then she recounted an ancient life that was so way out and "off the charts" that I would have dismissed it except for the fact that it related to what I was researching for *Past Shock* and this book:

> You are on a spaceship coming to Earth. You are frightened that you are going to be found out. You are part of a brotherhood that wants to help a newly created race of humans. As a kind of undercover agent, you plan to set these humans free of the oppressive religions that the human's creators had made for them. You know that these creators were not God, and that the claims they were making were false. It is a dangerous mission, and if you got caught you know that you will be put to death. This would be a horrible sentence, because at the time you had a life span of more than 10,000 years.

I asked Kirin what country this was, and she said "Sumeria."

I asked the time, and she claimed about 5,000 years ago.

I asked her one final question: "Was I ever found out?"

No.

Is this real? Is it the truth? Isn't this a little off the charts? To all three questions I answered, "I couldn't care less." It really doesn't matter whether it is true. What matters is what I experienced that night.

Whether truth, a significant metaphor, or simply a fiction to galvanize me, I wasn't the same after that night. That night ended my fourteen month period of doing nothing with writing about what happened thousands of years ago, that might be impacting us today.

As soon as I returned home, I turned on the word processor and brought up a file that I hadn't touched in fourteen months.

The file was called "Past Shock."

## *Past Shock: The Origin of Religion and Its Impact on the Human Soul. Book One.*

It was in the late 1960s, when Alvin Toffler coined the term "future shock"—a syndrome in which people are overwhelmed by the future. *Past Shock* suggests that events which happened thousands of years ago strongly impact humanity today. This book reveals the true reasons why religion was created, what organized religion won't tell you, the reality of the "slave chip" programming we all have to deal with, why we had to be created over and over again, what really happened in the Garden of Eden, what the Tower of Babel was and the reason why we were stopped from building it, how we were conditioned to remain spiritually ignorant, and much more. Jack exposes what he calls the "pretender gods", advanced beings who were not divine, but had advanced knowledge of scientific principles which included genetic engineering. Our advanced science of today has unraveled their secrets, and people like Barranger have the knowledge and courage to expose exactly how we were manipulated. Learn about our past conditioning and how to overcome the "slave chip" mentality in order to begin living life as it was meant to be, as a spiritually fulfilled being. ISBN 978-1-885395-085 * 132 pages * $12.95

**MYSTERIES EXPLORED:** *The Search for Human Origins, UFOs, and Religious Beginnings,* by Jack Barranger and Paul Tice. An overall investigation into human origins, religion, mythology, UFOs, and other unexplained phenomena. Begins by covering the most ancient mysteries about mankind and proceeds up to modern times, exploring the evidence, and ending with where we currently are from a religious and spiritual standpoint. A fascinating look at the development of mankind, with the possibility that we have experienced some form of "outside intervention" in remote times. In some ways, this intervention may still be with us today. **ISBN 1-58509-101-4 • 103 pages • 6 x 9 • perfect bound • $12.95**

---

*SPACE TRAVELERS AND THE GENESIS OF THE HUMAN FORM: Evidence of Intelligent Contact in the Solar System,* by Joan d'Arc. Can Darwinian evolution actually prove that we are alone in the Universe? This book illustrates that Darwinian evolution is not an empirically predictable or testable scientific paradigm. Also shows that ancient artifacts on Mars and the Moon are evidence of "Game Wardens" in our own solar system. Could the Earth be a controlled DNA repository for the ongoing creation and  dissemination of life forms, including humans? The author puts forth compelling evidence in this well researched work. **ISBN 1-58509-127-8 • 208 pages • $18.95**

---

*OF HEAVEN AND EARTH: Essays Presented at the First Sitchin Studies Day,* edited by Zecharia Sitchin. Contains further information on Sitchin's theories about the origins of mankind and the intervention of intelligence from beyond the Earth. He and the other contributors offer a scholarly approach to the ancient astronaut theory. Contains the complete transcript of the first Sitchin Studies Day, held in Denver, Colorado on Oct. 6, 1996. Following Sitchin's detailed keynote address are six other prominent speakers whose work he has influenced. They include philosopher Neil Freer, UFO expert J. Antonio Huneeus, clergyman Father Charles Moore, author V. Susan Ferguson, and two university professors, Madeleine Briskin and Marlene Evans. They agree that certain myths were actual events instead of figments of imaginations. Sitchin's work comprises the early part of a new paradigm—one that is already beginning to shake the very foundations of religion, archaeology and our society in general. **ISBN 1-885395-17-5 • 164 pages • 5 1/2 x 8 1/2 • perfect bound • illustrated • $14.95**